Privacy, Security, and Computers

O.E. Dial
Edward M. Goldberg

Privacy, Security, and Computers

Guidelines for Municipal and Other Public Information Systems

Praeger Publishers New York Washington London

PRAEGER SPECIAL STUDIES IN U.S. ECONOMIC, SOCIAL, AND POLITICAL ISSUES

Library of Congress Cataloging in Publication Data

Dial, O Eugene.
   Privacy, security, and computers: guidelines for
municipal and other public information systems.

   (Praeger special studies in U.S. economic, social,
and political issues)
   Bibliography: p.
   Includes index.
   1. Electronic data processing—Municipal government.
2. Electronic data processing departments—Security
measures.   3. Privacy, Right of—United States.
   I. Goldberg, Edward M., joint author.   II. Title.
   JS344.E4D5 1975   352'.94'1   74-13617
   ISBN 0-275-09890-7

PRAEGER PUBLISHERS
111 Fourth Avenue, New York, N.Y. 10003, U.S.A.
5, Cromwell Place, London SW7 2JL, England

Published in the United States of America in 1975
by Praeger Publishers, Inc.

Printed in the United States of America

This book was prepared under a Department of Housing and Urban Development contract with Long Island University for the Urban Information Systems Inter-Agency Committee (USAC) program. Neither the Department of Housing and Urban Development, the federal member agencies comprising the USAC Committee, nor the U. S. government in general makes any warranty, expressed or implied, or assumes responsibility for the accuracy or completeness of the information herein.

We wish to express our appreciation for the valuable assistance provided by the following people in the preparation of this manuscript. Donald Quigley, Operations Analyst, and Stewart Robinson, Computer Systems Specialist, both with the National Bureau of Standards, and Margaret (Peggy) Gooding and Richard Watson, both Government Technical Representatives in the USAC Office of the Department of Housing and Urban Development, for their critical reviews of the substantive material in the draft manuscript. Barbara Rosenthal, Administrative Assistant to the Municipal Information Systems Research Project, Long Island University, for her energetic, competent, and cheerful dedication to this work and Mary Kroehl, Secretary to the Graduate School of Public Affairs, University of Colorado, for her conscientious proofreading of the final manuscript.

We are deeply grateful to all of these people, but while we acknowledge their contributions, we remain solely responsible for the content of this report and any errors it may contain.

CONTENTS

LIST OF TABLES AND FIGURES

Privacy, Security, and Computers

This book has been prepared for city officials and concerned citizens. Its purpose is to bring to their attention a problem of increasing seriousness, one which affects them greatly, and to present a method of dealing with it: the problem is that of privacy in the computer age.

The threat to privacy has reached problem proportions with the increased use of computers at the municipal level and the concomitant storage of machine-readable data about the citizens and organizations under that jurisdiction. Though this may seem innocent, we are only now learning something of the possible degree of embarrassment to a city that fails to make explicit safeguards to protect its data and control the activities of its data processing unit. More specifically, the problem is to establish and maintain a balance between the public's "right to know" on the one hand and the citizen's "right to privacy" on the other.

SMALL VERSUS LARGE FACILITIES

Contrary to the popular impression, the smaller the scale of data processing activity, within limits, the greater the vulnerability of the city to data processing abuse. In a small operation each employee tends to perform in many roles; the same person may have access to the use of the computer, the programs, the files, and the forms (for example, blank checks). Combine this with the "after-hours" opportunity afforded in single shift operations, and we need only wait for a motive of sufficient strength to challenge the character of the employee. On the other hand, large operations have some degree of built-in protection because of the specialized roles played by their employees, their complexity, and their full-time utilization of the computer.

It is true that smaller operations handle data that are narrower in scope, although even here data and data processing typically include payroll, accounts payable, and property data. Furthermore, smaller operations tend to be informally supervised, with fewer written directives placing enforceable constraints upon the behavior of employees. Although large operations handle data that are wider in scope, their tendency to be more formally structured and supervised offsets to some degree the vulnerability caused by handling data of wider scope.

VULNERABILITY OF FACILITIES

Vulnerable to what? The Stanford Research Institute in its recently published report, Computer Abuse,[1] summarized 148 cases including such reports as theft of programs, fraud, embezzlement, alteration of records, vandalism, computer center destruction, extortion, programmed bigotry, theft of computers, forgery, theft of mailing lists, and removal of tape reel labels.

More significantly, most of the abuses against government computer centers occurred in local units of government.[2] The report points out that "collusion has a high frequency of occurrence, and the number of perpetrators is surprisingly large per case."[3]

Examples of abuses such as these are accumulating at a rate that parallels the growth in the use of computers. As shown by the Computerworld captions that are selected from issues published for a twelve-month period and listed in Table 1 one need only read this or other newspapers to learn of the growing concern for privacy and security in a computer environment; many more abuses undoubtedly have gone undetected. Implementing the procedures outlined in this handbook will do much to minimize the number and significance of these incidents.

This book, then, is about the problems of privacy and of data processing security and the methods by which these problems may be resolved. While we do not represent the subject as the greatest single problem facing cities today, we do seek to persuade city officials to recognize that the problem is there and that it must be dealt with rationally and expeditiously.

URBAN INFORMATION SYSTEMS, INTER-AGENCY COMMITTEE AND THE INTEGRATED MUNICIPAL INFORMATION SYSTEMS PROGRAM

Before continuing, however, it seems appropriate to discuss the program that has contributed the most significantly to an

TABLE 1

Privacy-Security-Computer-Related Material Reported in
Computerworld, December 1972 to December 1973

	Data	Page
Privacy		
"Critics Fear Privacy Invasion Under Bill for Drug Data Base"	12/6/72	36
"Computer Can Protect Privacy More than Jeopardize It"	12/13/72	4
"Privacy Issue Grows More Lively; Freeze Asked on LEAA Funds, Canada Forms Data Bank Unit, SS Number As UID in Doubt"	12/20/72	1
"Citizens' Committee Formed to Oversee Crime Net Privacy"	1/3/73	1
"Privacy—Common Ground Needed by All"	1/12/73	11-12
"ACPA Takes Privacy Stand; Forms Committee"	4/4/73	26
"Security, Privacy Major Parts of 'Q'; IBM Will Provide 'Tools'"	6/6/73	4
"Sound Policy Needed on Privacy and Data Security"	7/4/73	10
"Insufficiencies Cited at DP Centers; Societies Blast UK Census Security and Confidentiality"	8/1/73	6
"States Balk at U.S. Drug Plan, Say Privacy Rights Jeopardized"	8/15/73	1-2
Theft		
"Be Safe—Try to Break Your System"	6/6/73	1
"Girl Charged in Program Theft"	8/1/73	1,4
Fire		
"Security Checklist: Fire Prevention an Involved Process"	10/17/73	5
Power		
"Is Your Center's Power Supply Secure?"	10/3/73	9
General		
"Who Accesses What on Remote Terminal? DP Managers Must Have Stricter Control"	12/6/72	24
"T/S Vendors Stress Security of Terminal, Net, CPU"	12/6/72	21
"Users Awaken to Security Needs; FJCC Explores Data Protection, Guarding Centers Primary Concern"	12/6/72	1
"Security Device Market Still in Infancy"	12/6/72	1
"Multics Goes Commercial, Honeywell Pushes Security"	1/24/73	1,4
"IBM, Security Test Sites Vie on Software Strength"	6/13/73	1
"Part of an Insurance Program, Big-Time Security Analysis Needed"	6/29/73	19
"How Securely is your DP Center Built?"	10/31/73	6

Note: LEAA—Law Enforcement Assistance Agency SS—Social Security UID—Universal Identifier TS—Time Sharing FJCC — Fall Joint Computer Conference.

understanding of privacy and security at the municipal level, namely the Integrated Municipal Information Systems (IMIS) program of the federal Urban Information Systems Inter-Agency Committee (USAC). USAC was created in January 1969 to assist cities in the improvement of their information systems and hence management capabilities. Through this assistance the ability of cities to obtain, process, and use the information that is so vital to effective planning, management, and service would be enhanced. All of the federal agencies having programs that affected urban jurisdictions contributed representatives and other resources to plan and implement the first program of USAC, the IMIS program.[4]

This program was launched in July 1969, and by early 1970 contracts had been awarded to six cities. Two of the cities—Wichita Falls, Texas, and Charlotte, North Carolina—were to research and develop comprehensive integrated municipal information systems. Four cities were selected to research and develop integrated municipal information subsystems according to particular groupings of municipal functions, as indicated below:

Dayton, Ohio	Public Finance Information System (PFIS)
St. Paul, Minn.	Human Resources Development Information System (HRDIS)
Reading, Pa.	Physical and Economic Development Information System (PEDIS)
Long Beach, Calif.	Public Safety Information System (PSIS)

One of the basic objectives of the IMIS program was to research and develop a prototype that could be transferred with a minimum of modification to any city. While differences among cities would work against transfer, the similarities among cities with respect to the services they provide were much more in evidence, thus forming a basis for optimism about the feasibility of prototype transfer. To increase its transferability, project cities were required to develop the prototype with conventional hardware (computers and peripherals) and high-level, conventional software such as program listings together with explanatory remarks, detailed flow charts and systems design, data dictionaries, procedure listings, user manuals, and methods of development.

In addition to these projects, USAC recognized the need for research and development of the selected technologies upon which an operational information system would necessarily depend. The contracts with the IMIS cities therefore required research in such areas as geocoding, transferability, and data access control and confidentiality. The content of this book, in fact, rests heavily upon the thinking that went into the research design of IMIS, as updated by experiences in the IMIS cities.

The concern of USAC for the protection of individual privacy is readily apparent from the extracts from contract provisions set forth below:

> Much of the data circulating in a municipal information system are sensitive in that they relate to the private affairs of citizens, individually and collectively. While such data may be essential to planning other legitimate activities of a municipality, they may also serve the legitimate interests of other agencies and organizations. . . .
>
> To achieve these ends, while at the same time ensuring the maintenance of privacy for the individuals to whom the data relate, a Data Access Control Plan must be formulated and implemented. . . .
>
> *   *   *   *
>
> The Data Access Control Plan must make explicit the rules governing the release of data . . . in terms of who, what, when, and how. The plan must state who the authorized users are, what particular information may be released, and how, or at what level of aggregation.[5]

Further requirements provided for the flexibility and enforcement of the data access control plan and for the guidance, training, and supervision of the personnel who would participate in and implement the data access control plan.

DEVELOPMENTS IN THE USAC CITIES

By early 1974 the IMIS cities had generated a number of research reports and plans, and some of them had functioning data access control boards and had published sets of administrative regulations; all of these will of course be discussed in some detail in this handbook. Since the IMIS program was to continue into 1975, we may anticipate the availability of even more documentation in the area of privacy and security. Documents that are now available and that we feel will be most helpful in planning and implementing a system of data access control have been included in this book for purposes of illustration.[6]

ARRANGEMENT OF THIS BOOK

Following a general discussion of the developing problem of privacy and security, the reader will be led through a method of getting organized for data access control. This begins with the formulation of a plan that is best prepared within the city administration, although the impetus for it might originate with citizens or citizen groups. The plan shows the sequence in which the various documents must be prepared, the processes they must provide for, the people who will be required to participate in those processes, and the time allowances for each step of the way.

After the plan is completed, the first document provided for in the plan is prepared—the draft resolution recommended to the city council. This resolution creates an ad hoc data access control committee to become familiar with the subject and to make recommendations to the city council upon the completion of its study.

There follow three chapters dealing with special problems about which local decisions will need to be made, describing the nature of and need for software auditing and giving advice with respect to physical security control measures.

At this point the committee will have become familiar enough with the problem to draft and recommend the adoption of an ordinance creating a data access control board and assigning responsibilities and the resources necessary to discharge those responsibilities.

The final phase of the plan, the preparation and implementation of data access control administrative regulations, is then entered. These regulations provide in some detail for standards of data access control and security and for the procedures to implement those standards.

We stress the need for flexibility; the data access control board should have the authority to respond adequately to changing circumstances. The circumstance that is most certain to change is the volume and scope of public requests for data, as well as departmental requests for interdepartmental data. Both will increase markedly as the capabilities of an integrated data base come to be realized. Furthermore, flexibility will be needed to deal with the unanticipated questions that inevitably will arise.

A FUNDAMENTAL ASSUMPTION

We have made a fundamental assumption that affects virtually every chapter of this book. It is this: What constitutes an adequate measure of control over privacy and security is a local decision reflecting local attitudes, and may be expected to differ from city to city. It is in recognition of this that the book deals more with method than substance; in this spirit the models provided in the text are intended not as definitive last words but rather as useful points of departure.

In the final analysis, effective privacy and security controls for a municipal information system will be ensured by a concerned political leadership, by astute and dedicated management, by systems personnel who are aware and appreciative of privacy and security requirements, and by an informed public that will not tolerate illegal or unethical uses of a municipal information system.

American society wants and needs both better information systems and protection of individual privacy; these conflicting demands can be balanced rationally in the tradition of a free society. The opportunity to be creative and responsive is present; cities can meet the social challenges of the computer age individually as they develop their respective information systems. This book is intended to be helpful toward that end.

NOTES

1. Donn B. Parker et al, Computer Abuse: Final Report (Stanford, Calif.: Stanford Research Institute, November 1973).
2. Ibid., p. 41.
3. Ibid.
4. For a book-length discussion of USAC and the IMIS program, see Kenneth L. Kraemer et al., Integrated Municipal Information Systems: The Use of the Computer in Local Government (New York: Praeger Publishers, 1974).
5. Department of Housing and Urban Development (HUD) Requests for Proposal (RFP) H2=70, Attachment C, p. 32-34, as subsequently incorporated into contract with the IMIS cities.
6. For a listing of available documents see: A Bibliography of USAC Documentation, Municipal Systems Research Project, Claremont Men's College and Long Island University, Claremont, Ca., 1972. All documents are available through the National Technical Information Service (NTIS), U.S. Dept. of Commerce, Springfield, Va., 22151, or telephone 703-321-8888.

2

THE GROWING
RECOGNITION OF THE
PROBLEM OF PRIVACY

It is not new in our history for cities to assert the need, in fact the right, to information about its citizens. Nor is it new that beyond a certain point of divulgence, citizens resist providing further information about themselves, asserting the right to privacy. Furthermore, where personal information is provided to the city by the citizen, the citizen holds the city responsible for controlling access to that information. In other words it is the city's responsibility to assure and protect the citizens' privacy. In some instances the citizen also asserts the right to limit the city to using the information only for the purpose for which it was collected.

The basic conflict between the "right to know" and the "right to privacy" can be visualized as opposite poles of a continuum, a teeter-totter upon which right to know sits at one end and right to privacy sits at the other. The fulcrum of the teeter-totter will shift according to public mood, local conventions, and the effectiveness of the outbursts of the offended.

Accordingly, any system that deals with the resolution of these conflicts must be flexible and dynamic. It should be flexible to enable it to serve a variety of jurisdictions, each of which will want to locate its own fulcrum; and it should be dynamic in the sense that the fulcrum can shift, keeping the system abreast of changes in public attitudes.

The location of the fulcrum may shift or during some periods be fixed. This is usually accomplished by law—federal law, state statutes, and local ordinances. The usual approach is to make all public records available for inspection by citizens except for those records specifically identified by law as confidential; this suggests that in our culture there is a bias toward public disclosure of the information the government collects.

Local governments are creatures of the state. As such, their powers are defined by the state, and they must operate within the framework of state legislation. Every state in the Union has a "right to know" statute, which asserts that most public records must be open for inspection by anyone who wishes to view them.

The provisions of these statutes vary from state to state, but the intent of all such laws is clear: public business must be conducted publicly, and the people have the right to know what their governments are doing. For example, it would be impossible to guarantee even approximate fairness in the administration of property taxes if assessments were not matters of public record. The ability to inspect assessment records and to challenge assessments on the basis of factual knowledge of how comparable properties have been treated enables an individual to ensure that he is treated equitably in the taxation process.

However, other statutes provide that some records must remain strictly confidential. In many states, for example, adoption records, income tax records, and juvenile court records are defined as limited access records, which may not be revealed to any but authorized persons. In addition, in many states the courts have had occasion to interpret various statutes dealing with the public's right to know or the confidentiality of particular records. Local governments are of course bound by the provisions of state statutes and the state court decisions that interpret those statutes.

As will be seen, however, developments in computerized information systems have been so rapid and recent that state law and local ordinances have not caught up to the existing situation.

THE INFORMATION SYSTEMS REVOLUTION

If the 1960s can be regarded as the decade of the computer in America, surely it can be said that the 1970s will be regarded as the decade of information systems. More and more, both private and governmental organizations have turned to the use of computers. Local governments have joined this trend in an effort to enjoy its benefits of speed, accuracy, and efficiency.

But while earlier use of the computer was dedicated to computation and to sorting and listing tasks, its greater potential for information storage and processing was coming to be appreciated. It is with respect to this latter—information processing—that the wider implications, some of which are threatening to the privacy of citizens, have come to be realized.

This rapidly increasing reliance on computers has resulted in an information revolution. In joining this revolution, state and local governments should realize that many significant social issues accompany computerization.

THE NATURE OF THE DATA BASE

We live in a society that is increasingly dependent upon information. For a variety of reasons, an insatiable appetite has been developed for data about conditions, problems, and programs. An attempt to satisfy this appetite has led cities to go well beyond such a traditional use of computers as conventional finance applications and into the realm of information processing, which is the aggregating and correlating of data from diverse sources. This is necessary in order to have timely notice of municipal problems and information for monitoring, evaluating, and revising programs dealing with those problems. The computer and the data base in an information systems environment are integral to development of this capability.

This, then, has led to substantial increases in the dimensions and variety of data contained in the municipal data base, all in machine readable form. It also has led in varying degrees to the consolidation of the municipal data base under the dicta of a single rationalized scheme; this is known as the integration of the data base. The virtue of integration is that the content of the data base will be known and accessible at a central point, that is, at the data processing section.

The data contained in a modern integrated municipal information system comes from a wide variety of sources, including land title records; tax assessment and collection records; records of judgments and liens against real property; building inspection records; civil court records; police records; criminal and juvenile court records; health records, including hospital and clinical records of individuals; financial records, including tax payments of various kinds; inventories; and accounts receivable of municipally operated utilities or services.

The data generated in these records relates to individual citizens, businesses, and organizations, including addresses, phone numbers, and other identifying information regarding each. A significant portion, such as property tax assessments, has traditionally been regarded as matters of public record. However, different data have different levels of sensitivity. Some, such as patient medical records, relate to the private affairs of the individual, which other data affect the proprietary interests of business firms.

Much of the data contained in a municipal information system must be relatable to arbitrarily defined areas of the city in order to be useful. Otherwise it would not be possible to correlate data from jurisdictions whose borders are not conterminous. For example, it may be desirable to compare data from a school district with that of a police precinct, but the boundaries of each are usually quite different, thus rendering a comparison difficult. Problems of this kind are solved by arriving at a common denominator. This is usually a street address, although in many instances it may be the name of an individual. In either instance, the problem is solved by developing an ability to link the files of various jurisdictions and to search each in terms of the common denominator.

This is why an attempt is made in the development of a municipal information system to integrate the files in a manner that assures that they may be linked. By doing so the data may be applied to a much wider variety of uses. However, it is this very capability—file linkage—that exacerbates the problem of individual privacy. Data that individually may be matters of public record or have little sensitivity may in an integrated municipal information system be linkable to many other files containing data about the same people. Thus, should it be desired, a fairly complete picture of an individual can be obtained, one that in some instances would violate his desire for privacy. Through integrated file structures, dossier building by computer becomes possible.

THE ONGOING DEBATE

Security, the physical protection of computer facilities and of the information contained therein, had until the late 1960s been primarily a concern of commercial and military users of the computer. However, the threat to, and the protection of, personal privacy has since become a widely discussed public issue. A significant part of the literature of the computer world has been devoted to this subject. (See Bibliography.) These discussions can have substantial impact. For example, the defeat of the proposal to establish a National Data Center in 1966 is widely attributed to objections that the proposed center constituted a threat to personal privacy.

Privacy continues to be the focus of much attention by legislative bodies at all levels of government and by commentators in both the lay and computer press. Since 1971 discussion of privacy problems within the specific context of local government information systems has increased markedly, but the fact remains that the level of computerization has far exceeded the development of procedures for ensuring the maintenance of data access control.

Debate on both sides of the issue to date, with few exceptions, has been conducted largely on a superficial and emotional level, and this has not produced realistic solutions. In most instances the heat of the debate is explained by the failure of an agency to deal with the problem or to deal with it adequately, even though its information system may have been computerized for some length of time.

Ideally, the means of ensuring data access control, and hence privacy, should be developed well in advance of the development of

11

a computer-based information system. It may be argued that the development of the information system itself may be threatened thereby, and this is true; however, the dimension of the threat will be far more substantial should data access control not be addressed until after the privacy of citizens has been abused, as has been the usual case.

Many proponents of various types of information systems, both public and private, tend to pay lip service to the concept of personal privacy and to disregard the threats that are seen by critics. There are enough technical safeguards available, they correctly point out, that can be built into any information system for the protection of personal privacy and the confidentiality of the data contained in the system. They stress the potential and actual benefits of the system and the security that can be incorporated into both hardware and software.

Some critics appreciate both technology's usefulness and its threat to civil liberties; they stress the risks of misuse, abuse, negligence, insensitivity, bribery, and depersonalization that may accompany the development of a computerized information system, and they emphasize the need for the development of guidelines and regulations governing data collection and file confidentiality. However, many other critics tend to ignore or de-emphasize the potential usefulness of the system and stress the adverse potential of data surveillance. They emphasize, or perhaps overemphasize, the capacity of computers to build womb-to-tomb dossiers akin to the oral, visual, and written monitoring of human lives etched so sharply by George Orwell in his frightening novel 1984. At the very least there is a strong element of exploited fear in this perspective.

In addition, the computer has become a target in contemporary society for much of the discontent and alienation that afflicts many of our citizens. During many of the disturbances on American campuses in recent years, a favorite target of the demonstrators was the university computer center. We also have examples in the newspapers of fights with the computer by individuals; for example, a student at the University of California was photographed in a registration line wearing an oversized IBM card that read, "I am a human being—do not fold, spindle, or mutilate." There is little doubt that as more and more reliance on computers takes place, the image of an impersonal society is reinforced.

No matter how foolish these images appear to those who routinely work with computers, the fears are real, and they reflect a legitimate concern about the potential loss of personal identity and privacy. Those in government are well advised to anticipate, understand, and be responsive to these fears. Local governments in particular, being closest to their citizens and having more information about them on record, have a particular obligation to assure adequate measures of data access control in their information systems.

12

Furthermore, a municipal information system constitutes a very real threat to personal privacy, which is the ability of an individual to control the circulation of information relating to himself. As the efficiency and scope of the information system increases, the threat to personal privacy becomes greater. This in turn results in increased public concern and discussion about the potential deleterious effects of computerization. The fact that these concerns are often exaggerated and carried by rumor by no means relieves the municipality of the responsibility for putting them to rest. To intensify this public concern, there have been sufficient instances in which these rumors have been found to be true.

Being responsive to the legitimate concerns of individuals does not mean abandoning efforts to develop computerized information systems for local government. Nor does it mean abandoning plans to widen the scope of the data base and make it more accessible through its integration.

Most people recognize that the information activities of local governments are legitimate and necessary, and that the use of computers can contribute greatly toward improving the quality of life in our cities. The ability to gather, process, integrate, and analyze data improves the ability of municipal governments to define problems and to develop solutions for them. A deeper understanding of the problems that must be faced in the area of privacy and data confidentiality is needed, particularly because the existing practices, procedures, and conventions are disturbed by conversion from manual to computerized systems.

Since conflicting claims and values are often present, the balance between them needs to be rationalized and understood. The purpose of the following chapters is to describe the procedures that will enable a city to cope with these conflicts within the framework of local considerations, that is to say, within its own unique situation.

13

3

PLANNING DATA
ACCESS CONTROL

The development and implementation of data access control involves the making of a number of policy decisions, the preparation of a number of important documents, the implementation of a number of processes, and the assignment of roles to individuals who will participate in these processes.

In the aggregate, data access control is time-valued and complex enough to require planning. Development of a plan requires substantial effort, since the plan anticipates and sequences the required steps in a logical order, identifies individuals who will be required for the accomplishment of each step, sets time frames for each step, and otherwise assures the rational development and implementation of data access control. The data access control plan must be sufficiently flexible to permit adaptation to changing circumstances, such as policy decisions relating to changing time frames or the consolidation or division of particular documents and processes provided for in the plan.

Because of the need for professional attention and continuity of responsibility for the preparation and implementation of the plan, it is advised that the plan be prepared by a member of the staff of the city administrator, under his direction. A member of the staff of the city administrator is also in the best position to monitor developments on a continuing basis; to advise the administrator of the status of the plan from time to time; to alert the administrator when action is required that is beyond the jurisdiction of the administrator; and in time, as the plan begins to be implemented, to assume the role of data access control supervisor (or monitor or coordinator, according to the particular title selected).

The products, processes, and roles that contribute to the achievement of data access control will be discussed in some detail in the chapters to follow, but here we are concerned with the development

of a plan to create them. Therefore the discussion of each in the
sections to follow will be limited to the perspective of plan development.

PRODUCTS

The plan should provide for developing the following documents,
in the order listed:

1. A draft resolution appropriate for adoption by the city council should be prepared. This resolution is the first official expression
of interest by the city in assuring: (a) adequate security for the data
it collects; (b) limitation and control of access to that data; (c) protection of the privacy of the citizens in its jurisdiction; and (d) as-
surance of access by citizens to public records. The primary purpose
of the draft resolution is to appoint an ad hoc committee to study the
problem and to construct an ordinance appropriate for dealing with
it, one that can be recommended to the city council for consideration.

2. A legal study should be prepared as the first effort of the
ad hoc committee on data access control. The committee will require
staff support by the administrator, together with substantial assistance
from the city attorney, in the production of this study. The study
should contain the results of a search of the law—federal, state, and
local—in order to be thoroughly and accurately advised of the authority
and responsibility of the city and of the limitations on that authority
and responsibility to act in this subject area. Emphasis should be
on two areas, citizens' rights to access to public records and citizens'
rights to privacy with respect to selected records. The study should
provide descriptions of the records in each category. It should con-
clude with a preliminary assessment of the extent to which the law
is being satisfied by current operating procedures.

3. A draft ordinance appropriate for adoption by the city council should then be prepared. This ordinance is an outgrowth of a draft
ordinance prepared by the staff of the ad hoc committee. Because of
the range of provisions the draft ordinance contains, the committee
will be required to make a number of policy decisions, some of which
will be at variance with the ordinance the staff has prepared; thus
the ordinance may proceed through many drafts before reaching the
recommending or hearing stage.

Experience indicates that there is a constant temptation for
the committee to bog down in specific and sometimes tangential issues. For this reason the committee staff should exercise initiative
in preparing the agenda for each meeting, highlighting those decision
points that are important enough for the committee's attention and
indicating the volume of work to be accomplished. This also assures

15

that the subject matter will be developed systematically within the scheduled time frame and that the desired document will ultimately be produced.

The ordinance differs from the resolution in that it authorizes and directs the city administration, or specific offices within it, to assume a defined range of responsibilities on a continuing basis. It also creates a permanent data access control board to exercise monitoring, revision of the rules within limits, and appellate authority where the rulings of subordinates in the system are challenged by citizens. Finally, the ordinance should stipulate penalties for noncompliance.

4. Administrative regulations stipulate the rules by which the ordinance will be implemented. The rules are specific in their provisions, while the ordinance is general. One of the offices created by the ordinance is that of data access control supervisor (or a variation of the same title), and this responsibility is assigned to a member of the city administration. One of the first duties of the supervisor is to develop a set of administrative regulations designed to implement the spirit and substance of the data access control ordinance. After review and approval by the data access control board, the regulations are promulgated within the city administration and implemented. The regulations should stipulate penalties for noncompliance within the authority contained in the data access control ordinance.

5. A statement of ethics should be developed and incorporated into the administrative regulations. This statement of ethics should be promulgated to data processing personnel and all others in the city administration having responsibility for information handling. The statement should reflect the spirit and intent, expressed in general terms, of the data access control ordinance and administrative regulations. While all members of the city administration cannot be expected to be cognizant of all provisions of the lengthy and complex administrative regulations, except for those portions governing their own respective duties, all members can be expected to be familiar with, and guided and alerted by, the relatively short and simple statement of ethics. These, in fact, are the distinguishing characteristics of the two documents.

PROCESSES

The purpose of generating the documents discussed above is not only to set overall standards of data access control but also to set in motion the processes that will be required to make the system effective on a continuing basis. The most important of these processes are discussed below.

1. Policy generation is an ongoing requirement. Changes will be necessary to interpret existing standards and to meet new circumstances with the generation of new standards or the modification of old ones.

2. Monitoring the data access control system is required at all levels, from that of the data access control board on down, on a continuing basis. This may take the form of periodic inspections, of random inspections in point of time or segment of the system, or of provisions for independent audits by experts beyond the city administration.

3. Arbitration of conflict will be required from time to time, particularly as administrators at the same level, or the city administration vis-a-vis a citizen or organization in the community, differ about the accessibility of desired data.

4. Updating the administrative regulations will be an ongoing task, not only to meet new circumstances but to more effectively guide the system in existing circumstances as potential improvements are recognized.

ROLES

In the construction of his plan, the data access control planner will need at the outset some notion of the various people and roles that will be required in the development and implementation of the system of data access control. Having listed the roles to be performed and made tentative assignments of persons appropriate to those roles, he will need to associate the roles with the preparation of particular documents. The following list is suggested as a point of departure:

1. Data access control plan — a member of the city administration who reports directly to the city administrator and as advised by liaison with all those listed below

2. Draft resolution — data access control planner
city administrator
city attorney
city council

3. Ad hoc committee membership — city administrator
data access control planner (nonvoting staff support)
city attorney (nonvoting staff support)
two city administration department heads

	two private citizens, each representing a competing interest in obtaining or protecting the privacy of information, such as the media and the American Civil Liberties Union
4. Legal study	ad hoc committee committee staff city attorney
5. Draft ordinance	ad hoc committee committee staff city attorney city council
6. Data access control supervisor	as designated, but preferably the data access control planner
7. Data access control board membership	city administrator city attorney (nonvoting staff support) data access control supervisor (nonvoting staff support) three city administration department heads three private citizens, each representing a competing interest in obtaining or protecting information
8. Administrative regulations	data access control supervisor city administrator data processing chief city personnel officer data access control board city attorney (review and advise)
9. Statement of ethics	data access control supervisor city administrator data processing chief data access control board city attorney (review and advise)

TIME

Experience indicates that, given the opportunity, the development and implementation of a data access control system will require two to three years or perhaps forever. Many reasons are advanced in justification of this exceedingly great length of time: (1) the nature of and need for data access control is neither widely understood nor appreciated, and thus time must be allowed for the orientation of the community, including citizens and political leaders and administrators; (2) the pioneering nature of the subject, particularly at the local level, allows few precedents by which to be guided; (3) there is a constant tendency of boards and committees to get sidetracked on minor or tangential issues, thus failing to come to grips with the overall appearance of the system to be devised; (4) there is a tendency to give the subject a lower priority for development when faced with issues that are perceived locally as more critical in nature; and finally (5) a plan has not been devised for the development of the system in which each element of the development has been set along a time line, that is, scheduled.

However, it should be noted that many of the conditions discussed above have changed. The nature of and need for data access control are widely discussed: this is demonstrated by the dissemination of books and articles on the subject and the increasing appearance in the media of instances in which data processing systems have been penetrated by unauthorized persons or abused by city personnel. We now have a few examples of data access control systems, together with the documentation of those systems. Finally, it is hoped that the contents of this book may be of assistance in guiding cities through the development and implementation of a data access control system.

There is therefore no longer a need for a time allowance of two or three years to develop a system. In devising the data access control plan, reasonable periods of time should be allowed for the accomplishment of each step in the development of the system, and development should be closely monitored with a view to adhering to these time allowances. Communicating these allowances to boards and committees should make them aware of the importance of keeping within the time allotted.

The ability to keep to the planned schedule will necessitate competent and timely staff work. Where a data access control planner is assigned on a full-time basis, there should be every expectation of developing and implementing the system within a period of six months.

The purpose of this chapter has primarily been to stress the importance of looking at a generalized model of the entire system, then of breaking it into its parts and sequencing and scheduling the development of those parts. In the chapters to follow we will go into much greater detail about the content of each part; by this we hope to provide a sufficient point of departure toward the development of a system that can be uniquely appropriate to each city.

4

PRELIMINARY WORK

THE NEED FOR A DRAFT RESOLUTION

It may be argued that a draft resolution is unnecessary, that a city may proceed directly to an ordinance creating a data access control board and equipping it with the powers and responsibilities needed to develop a functioning data access control system. We recommend otherwise, however, because the typical city has had little experience with data access control and the resolution stage provides an opportunity to approach the subject from the beginning. It is important to collect convincing evidence that there really is a need for a formal data access control system and to publicize that need in the community. Unless the need is fully appreciated in the political, administrative, and other sectors of the city, it is doubtful that further action will be taken.

The need should not be assumed nor based entirely upon authoritative publications; it must be established and defined in terms of the federal, state, and local law having application in a particular city and by an assessment of the attitudes with respect to rights or privacy prevailing in a particular community. It is then necessary to evaluate the existing system of data access control for its adequacy in satisfying the requirements, which by then have been made explicit.

All of this is best accomplished by a small group of citizens assisted by the city attorney and a professional public administrator, namely the committee created by the resolution. Some cities will prefer that this background work be performed more efficiently. However, containing the effort within the administration overlooks the need to include the community in understanding and solving the problems of data access control. Furthermore, it is doubtful that the range of attitudes represented in diverse segments of the community can be anticipated adequately without private-citizen participation.

It should be kept in mind that the resolution stage is only a preliminary step; it makes no continuing commitment of any kind, but merely establishes a temporary committee to look into and become familiar with the subject and thereafter to advise whether or not a permanent data access control board should be formed, to establish and govern a data access control system.

It should also be kept in mind that resources will be needed to develop and implement a data access control system; given the competition for municipal resources, the system should not be developed unless the need is substantial and competes favorably with other needs in the city. The committee can do much in its investigations to establish whether or not the system is needed and what priority should be attached to its development. Both questions, in our view, need to be answered with conviction before the ordinance stage of development is reached.

THE RESOLUTION

There are many variations possible in framing an adequate resolution, but the one that is set forth here will serve as a point of departure in drafting one for your particular city.

A Resolution
Creating an Ad Hoc Data Access Control Committee

WHEREAS, the City of _____ respects the tradition of visibility of government; and,

WHEREAS, this tradition is furthered by making public records available for inspection by citizens; and,

WHEREAS, this City respects the tradition of protecting the rights of citizens to privacy with respect to personal information which the city collects and files; and,

WHEREAS, the increasing use of automated data processing the administration of municipal affairs has a potential for disturbing the continuation of the foregoing traditions;

NOW, THEREFORE, BE IT RESOLVED BY THE CITY COUNCIL OF THE CITY OF _____, THAT:

Section 1. The Mayor shall establish an Ad Hoc Data Access Control Committee to examine the requirements for and status of Data Access Control in the City administration, to reach such conclusions as may be warranted, and to recommend to the City Council such action as then seems appropriate.

Section 2. The Committee shall be composed of the City Manager, as Chairman, together with the following members:

a. A professional public administrator from within the City Administration who shall serve as Data Access Control Planner to provide non-voting staff support to the Committee on a full-time basis.

b. The City Attorney (nonvoting staff support).

c. Two senior members of the City Administration.

d. Two private citizens, one of whom shall represent that sector of the community interested in obtaining information, and the other representing that sector of the community interested in protecting the privacy of information.

Section 3. The specific duties of the Committee shall be as follows:

a. To research the federal, state, and local laws with respect to accessibility of information collected and filed by the city.

b. To research the available literature with respect to data access control in an automated data processing environment.

c. To assess the expectations of local citizens with respect to accessibility and privacy of information collected and filed by the municipality.

d. To examine the existing system of data access control in terms of all of the foregoing.

e. To set forth such findings as the investigation may warrant.

f. To make such recommendations to the City Council as seem appropriate to the Committee, in particular with reference to the following questions:

1) Is the existing system of data access control adequate?

2) Should the City develop and implement a formal system of data access control?

3) Should the City establish a permanent Data Access Control Board to develop and supervise the implementation and operation of a formal system of data access control?

g. To draft an ordinance appropriately reflective of the recommendations of the Committee for consideration by the City Council.

Section 4. The City Manager is directed to provide such clerical support as the Committee may require in the conduct of its work.

Section 5. It is desired that the Committee complete its work and report its findings, conclusions, and recommendations within a period of forty-five days from the date of this resolution.

THE LEGAL STUDY

The most natural division of the preliminary research effort is made by requiring a legal study by the city attorney, while the remainder of the preliminary research is done by the data access control planner assigned to provide staff support to the committee.

In view of the attention this subject has gained in the literature, in state legislatures, and in the Congress, the city attorney will be well advised to examine not only existing law but also bills that are currently under consideration. In April 1973 the Computer and Business Equipment Manufacturers Association tabulated and summarized all bills under consideration in state legislatures that affected privacy. As shown on Table 2, they were able to list some thirty bills, under consideration in 18 states.

The National Bureau of Standards prepared a similar list with respect to federal legislation for its Conference on Privacy and Computer Security on November 19 and 20, 1973, Washington, D.C. Table 3 shows that three bills have been enacted and nine are presently under consideration in either the House or the Senate.[1]

Not only is federal legislation often used as a model for state legislation, hence to be examined critically, but some of this legislation directly affects the city. For example, H. R. 188, providing for the dissemination and use of criminal arrest records in a manner that insures their security and privacy, would affect all states and cities participating in the Computerized Criminal History network of the National Crime Information Center. This legislation would set forth stringent rules for the management and operation of local computer centers having access to the network. Compliance with those rules would be a condition of participation in the network.

Finally, it is important not only to research and summarize existing law, but where possible to provide interpretation of that law to the committee. The research conducted by the Municipal Information Systems Department in Charlotte, North Carolina, as set forth in Table 4, provides a useful example of the variety of titles under which applicable state law may be found.

TABLE 2

State Legislation—Privacy and Security, April 27, 1973

Alaska (HCR44)[a] Study Commission to recommend how the new State
constitutional provision guaranteeing the people's right to
privacy should be implemented. Recommended for passage.
Adjournment 4/7. Bills carry over.

Arizona (SB1248)[a] providing that processing and keeping of public
records may be contracted out and regulating the disclosure
of tax information handled by a data processing organization.
Reported from Fin./Rev. Comm. 3/12. In Rules.

California (AB39)[a] Establishment of a criminal code. Chapter 3 of
which is entitled "privacy," but relates primarily to communications. Hearings: 4/25-5/2.

California (AB800)[b] Regulation of Consumer Reporting Agencies.
Finance and Insurance Committee. Hearing 5/2.

California (SB334) Extends professional privilege to cover communication for accounting purposes. Passed Senate 4/12.

Colorado (H1539)[b] regulation of consumer reporting agencies.

Georgia (HB593) Allows communication of tax information for data
processing purposes and subjects recipient to controls.

Hawaii (HB1604) This is a strange bill addressing many facets of
privacy protection in its purpose section, but reciting no means.
In Committee on Human Rights and Judiciary. Legislature
adjourned 4/26. Bills carry over.

Hawaii (HB1936)[b] Temporary Legislative Commission on the Social
Uses of Computer Technology. Judiciary and Finance Committee. Legislature adjourned 4/26, Bills carry over.

Illinois (HB468, HB4659) Establishes and funds Right of Privacy
Commission.

Illinois (H743 and S360)[b] Creates Data Information Study Commission.
S360 recommended for passage 4/24. H743 Hearing 4/27—
Executive Committee.

Indiana (SB234) Use of electronic data processing systems in the
keeping of hospital medical records.

Iowa (S115)[b] regulating Disclosure of Criminal History and Intelligence
Data. Passed Senate 3/9; Passed House 4/13. Bill much
amended.

Maryland (HB150) Amend Declaration of Rights to state that the right
of privacy shall not be abridged without due process. Adjourned
4/9.

Massachusetts (H1417) Establishes the Massachusetts Privacy Board
and guarantees the privacy of certain records.

Massachusetts (H2937) Establishing a special commission relative to
invasions of privacy.

Minnesota (S1045) Regulates the collection, security and dissemination of state records.

Minnesota (H450) Requiring Credit Bureaus to disclose records on demand of their subject.

Minnesota (H569) Allows one who prepares tax returns for others to further disclose that information to obtain computer services.

Minnesota (H1316)[b] Control of collection, security and dissemination of records and information by the State.

Montana (H616)[b] Regulation of Consumer Reporting Agencies.

New York (A622, A6072, S2642) Provides access to credit bureau reports.

New York (A1510, S3102) Same as Congressman Koch's Government Records Control bill (HR854).

New York (A6668) (Copy not yet received) Requiring consumer reporting agencies to meet confidentiality, accuracy and relevancy standards.

New York (S4581)[b] regulate those who collect credit data.

New York (S4804)[b] Permit individuals access to information relating to them held by the division of criminal justice services.

New York (A6929)[b] To regulate computer controlled billing procedures.

New Jersey (SCR12) Creating a commission to study the matter of invasion of personal privacy.

New Jersey (A2154) Fair Credit Billing Act, very similar to Senator Proxmire's bill.

Oregon (S616) Creating a Data Processing Advisory Commission, one of the duties being to advise regarding security factors.

Vermont (JRS 17) Establishing a Commission on Information to study all aspects of information gathering and utilization. Referred to Government Operations 2/23.

Washington (H720, S2595)[a] Establishing state data processing authority including the duty to maintain the confidentiality of data. Legislature adjourned 4/16. Bills carry over to special session scheduled for September 8.

---

[a]indicates changes in status
[b]indicates new bill

Source: Computer and Business Equipment Manufacturers Association, 1973.

TABLE 3

Federal Legislation on Privacy and Security

Freedom of Information Act (5 U.S.C. 552) provides for making information
   held by federal agencies available to the public unless it comes within
   one of the specific categories of matters exempt from public disclosure.
   Enacted.

Federal Reports Act (44 U.S.C. 3501) establishes procedures for the collection
   of information by federal agencies and the transfer of confidential information from one agency to another. Enacted.

Fair Credit Reporting Act (15 U.S.C. 1681) requires consumer reporting agencies to adopt procedures which are fair and equitable to the consumer
   with regard to the confidentiality, accuracy, relevancy and proper use
   of such information. Enacted.

(S.B. 2200) govern the disclosure of certain financial information by financial
   institutions to governmental agencies to protect the constitutional rights
   of citizens of the U.S. and to prevent unwarranted invasions of privacy
   by prescribing procedures and standards governing disclosure of such
   information. Banking, Housing and Urban Affairs.

(S.J. Res. 124) to establish a Joint Committee on Individual Rights. Judiciary
   Committee referral.

(H.R. 188) to amend Title 28 of the U.S. Code to provide for the dissemination
   and use of criminal arrest records in a manner that insures their security and privacy. Judiciary Committee referral.

(H.R. 665) to protect the constitutional rights of U.S. citizens and to prevent
   unwarranted invasions of privacy by prescribing procedures and stan-
   da rds governing the disclosure of information to government agencies.
   Banking, Currency Committee referrals.

(H.R. 667) to amend Title 5 of the U.S. Code to provide that persons be ap-
   prised of records concerning them that are maintained by government
   agencies. Government Operations referral.

(H.R. 4960) to amend section 552 of Title 5 of the U.S. Code (Freedom of Information Act) to limit exemptions to disclosures of information, to
   establish a Freedom of Information Commission, and to further amend
   the Act. Government Operations referral.

(H.R. 10042) to provide standards of fair personal information practices.
   Judiciary Committee referral.

(H.R. 9786) to assure the constitutional right of privacy by regulating automatically processed files identifiable to individuals by the creation of
   a Federal Privacy Board, to establish limitations on data which can be
   stored, and provide for criminal sanctions and civil liability. Judiciary
   Committee referral.

(H. Res. 606) to create a Select Committee on Privacy to conduct investigations
   of all aspects of privacy invasion, including data banks and related activities. Rules Committee referral.

Note: This listing is intended to be an indication of Congressional concerns. It is not a comprehensive list of all legislation enacted or introduced
on this subject.

TABLE 4

North Carolina Statutes on Privacy and Security

<hr>

Public Records, Chapter 132

132.1 Public records defined - Public records comprise all written or printed books, papers, letters, documents and maps made and received in pursuance of law by the public offices of the State and its counties, municipalities and other subdivisions of government in the transaction of public business.

132.2 Custodian designated - The public official in charge of an office having public records shall be the custodian thereof.

132.3 Destruction of records regulated - No public official may destroy, sell, loan, or otherwise dispose of any public record, except in accordance with 121.5, without the consent of the State Department of Archives and History.

132.6 Inspection and examination of records - Every person having custody of public records shall permit them to be inspected and examined at reasonable times and under his supervision by any person, and he shall furnish certified copies thereof on payment of fees as prescribed by law.

132.7 Keeping records in safe places; copying or repairing; certified copies - Insofar as possible, custodians of public records shall keep them in fireproof safes, vaults, or rooms fitted with non-combustible materials and in such arrangement as to be easily accessible for convenient use. All public records should be kept in the buildings in which they are ordinarily used . . . Any public official who causes a record book to be copied shall attest it and shall certify on oath that it is an accurate copy of the original book. The copy shall then have the force of the original.

132.9 Violation of chapter a misdemeanor - Any public official who refuses or neglects to perform any duty required of him by this chapter shall be guilty of a misdemeanor.

Adoption, Chapter 48

48.25 (a) Neither the original file of the proceeding in the office of the clerk nor the recording of the proceeding by the State Board of Public Welfare shall be open for general public inspection.
(b) With the exception of the information contained in the final order, it shall be a misdemeanor for any person having charge of the file or the record to disclose, except as provided in G.S. 48.26, and as may be required under the provisions of G.S. 48.27, any information concerning the contents of any papers in the proceeding.
(c) No director of public welfare or any employee of a public welfare department nor a duly licensed child placing agency or any of its employees shall be required to disclose any information, written or verbal, relating to any child or to its natural, legal or adoptive parents . . . except by order of the clerk of the superior court. . . .

Employment Security Commission, Chapter 96

96.4 (g) Records and Reports- -
(1) Each employing unit shall keep true and accurate employment records containing such information as the Commission may prescribe. Such records shall be open to inspection and be subject to being copied by the Commission . . . The Commission may require from any employing unit any sworn or unsworn reports, with respect to persons employed by it . . . Information thus obtained shall not be published or be open to public inspection (other than to public employees in the performance of their public duties) in any manner revealing the employing unit's identity . . . Any employee or member of the Commission who violates any provision of this section shall be fined not less than twenty dollars ($20.00) nor more than two hundred dollars ($200.00), or imprisoned for not longer than ninety days or both. . . .

(Continued)

TABLE 4 (Continued)

Board of Public Welfare, Chapter 108

108.14.2   The said lists showing the names, addresses and amounts of public assistance paid to each individual . . . are hereby declared to be public records and shall be open to public inspection at all times during the regular office hours of said auditor. . . . The names of and the salaries paid to all employees of the county board of public welfare are hereby declared to be public records. . . .

108.14.4   Except as provided in this article, it shall be unlawful for any person, firm, or corporation, board, body, association or other agency of any kind whatsoever to solicit, disclose, receive, make use of, any list or lists of names or any list of names derived from the reports provided for by this article for commercial or political purposes of any nature. . . .

Department of Social Service, Chapter 108

108.45   (a) Except as provided in (b) below, it shall be unlawful for any person to obtain, disclose or use, or to authorize, permit, or acquiesce in the use, of any list of names or other information concerning persons applying for or receiving public assistance. . . .
(b) The Department of Social Services shall furnish a complete list of names, addresses, and amounts of monthly grants of all persons receiving payments under all programs . . . to the auditor of each county at least semiannually. This list shall be a public record open to inspection. . . . The list, or any part of it, may not be published in any newspaper or periodical nor used for any commercial or political purpose. . . .

Juvenile Courts, Chapter 110

110.24   . . . The court shall maintain a full and complete record of all cases brought before it. . . . All records may be withheld from indiscriminate public inspection in the discretion of the judge of the court, but such record shall be open to inspection by the parents, guardians, or other authorized representatives of the child concerned.

The Blind, Chapter 111

111.28   It shall be unlawful, except for purposes directly connected with the administration of aid to the needy blind and in accordance with the rules and regulations of the State Commission for the Blind, for any person or persons to solicit, disclose, receive, make use of, or authorize, knowingly permit, participate in, or acquiesce in the use of, any list of or name of, or any information concerning, persons listed in the register of the blind.

Real Estate Assessment Books, Chapter 160

160.100   The city clerk or person designated shall prepare . . . a well bound book . . . to show: (1) Name of owner of such property
(2) The number or lot . . .
(3) The frontage of said lot
Such book shall . . . be open to the inspection of any citizen of the municipality.

Municipal Meetings, Chapter 160

160.269   The city governing body shall from time to time establish rules for its proceedings. . . . All legislative sessions shall be open to the public, and every matter shall be put to a vote, the result of which shall be duly recorded. . . . A full and accurate journal of the proceedings shall be kept, and shall be open to the inspection of any qualified registered voter of the city.

Source: City of Charlotte, Municipal Information Systems Department, Charlotte, N.C. 1972.

FURTHER RESEARCH

The weight of the remaining preliminary research should fall upon the data access control planner. This will consist primarily of three tasks: (1) a close review of the selected material contained in the annotated bibliography in this book and whatever other useful materials he may find; (2) a survey of community expectations with respect to privacy; and (3) a review and assessment of the existing system of data access control in the city.

With respect to the first task, it should be noted that even though we have been highly selective of the material placed in the bibliography it nonetheless is more than can reasonably be expected to be read by each member of the committee. On the other hand, it would be helpful if the planner could brief the committee on materials he finds to be significant, perhaps supplementing the briefing with written summaries, and providing such additional details or answers as the committee may require.

For the second task, community expectations with respect to privacy are most easily gleaned from a review of newspaper items published in the past few years. Have there been complaints? Court cases? Editorials? This effort can be supplemented by interviews with leaders of the media and business and with a few prominent citizens, all of whom can be presumed to contribute to the formulation of public opinion.

The leaders of civic groups and research institutes, such as may be found on college campuses, should also be interviewed. Are their requests to the city for data being satisfied? Finally, officers within the city administration should be interviewed in order to discover the types of information typically requested by others and to learn whether or not such requests are granted.

This kind of research yields no firm quantitative measurement, but it does result in a feel for the situation. It enables the researcher to decide whether, in general, community expectations for information are being met and to ascertain the level of confidence in the city's efforts to protect the confidentiality of personal information. These evaluations should enable the committee to assess the risk of maintaining the status quo as opposed to taking remedial measures.

The data access control planner has by now obtained the results of the legal study, completed his assessment of community expectations, and become familiar with the remaining material in this book, particularly the next three chapters. The planner is now ready for the third preliminary task, to evaluate the existing data access control system in terms of these requirements. Checkoff lists are provided in some of the material referenced at the end of the next three chapters;

29

these should be helpful in evaluating the existing system. However, an evaluation in those terms alone would, for obvious reasons, be incomplete.

The evaluation will not be easy, primarily because of the informality with which the systems of most cities function. It will be difficult, if possible at all, to find written regulations on the subject. The usual convention observed is that the office that originates the data controls its release. On the other hand, the planner may find that some departments, for selected categories of data, allow the discretion of the data processing chief to be controlling. Since these procedures result from oral arrangements that are rarely put down on paper, the research will necessarily proceed by personal interview with the city manager, each department head, and the data processing chief.

The evaluation should also entail a physical inspection of the data processing facilities. It is here that the checkoff lists can be most helpful, but even so, judgment must be exercised in evaluating the significance of unsatisfactory marks on the checkoff list. The literature research should equip the planner to make such judgments.

THE WORK OF THE COMMITTEE

The committee should meet frequently, that is, weekly, during the resolution phase in the development of a data access control system. This is to enable the committee members to be familiar with the results of the research while it is in progress. By the fourth of these sessions the committee should be able to hear the results of the evaluation of the existing system. It is following that session that the real work of the committee will begin, namely, arriving at a consensus regarding the facts, conclusions, and recommendations it must report.

The deck of reading material is loaded: if the city is average in most respects a sense of alarm will begin to be felt. The potential liability of the city and the dimensions of the risk that is currently being run become abundantly clear, and the committee will in all probability opt for the creation of a data access control board and the development and implementation of a formal system of data access control. The committee will then begin to draft the ordinance to be recommended for consideration by the city council.

Before discussing the contents of the draft ordinance, however, we should pause to consider the material contained in the next three chapters, since the committee will need to make decisions with respect to this material before drafting the ordinance. The primary decision is how much of the material, if any, should be frozen into an ordinance, on the one hand, and how much should be reserved for decision by the data access control board and subsequently promulgated in administrative regulations. Obviously, flexibility is maximized by the latter course of action, which leaves the board free to cope with changing circumstances. We will return to the task of drafting the ordinance in Chapter 8.

NOTE

1. For a listing and summary of other bills and resolutions which are relevant see Linda Flato, "Behind the Privacy Bill," Computer Decisions, September 1974, p. 26.

5

SPECIAL PROBLEM AREAS

The purpose of this chapter is to identify a range of problem areas and some considerations that are relevant to these problems, rather than to suggest substantive solutions, which seem warranted for several reasons. First, there are no simple solutions, other than procedural, to the problems that may arise when a city converts its manual records to an automated system. It simply is not possible to anticipate all of the tensions that will arise between the public's right to know and the individual's right to privacy. Furthermore, the powers, structures, and attitudes of local governments vary from state to state and within the same state, and hence the ability and desire of the local government to deal with problems of privacy will vary substantially.

On the other hand, while no state has a comprehensive information-handling statute at this time, there is a growing body of useful precedents. These precedents take the form of numerous bills now under consideration by various legislatures[1] and also of the studies, reported resolutions, ordinances, and regulations having to do with privacy that have been published by the cities developing Integrated Municipal Information Systems (IMIS) under contracts with USAC.[2]

There is by now sufficient experience with various types of information systems, in government at all levels and in the private sector, to enable us to identify some common problems and some considerations that are relevant to those problems. This in itself is useful because the anticipation of these problems will help shape a system of procedures that can in turn be responsive to them.

COLLECTION OF DATA

It should come as no surprise that most city governments do not know the full range of the data they collect and therefore cannot know the extent of the personal or otherwise sensitive data that they collect about their citizens. The first step for a city in discovering the extent of this problem is to conduct a study throughout the municipal administration that answers these questions: What data are being collected by the city? What offices are collecting them? By what authority are they being collected? Are the data collected essential to the performance of authorized municipal functions?

This study is usually approached by conducting an inventory of all forms in use and by examining each form to discover its originating office, content, purpose, authority, and level of sensitivity. This information is then studied in aggregate in order to learn the amount of duplication in data collection that exists and to get some sense of the levels of data sensitivity and associated safeguards that ought to be established.

The question of who puts what data into the system, and under what circumstances, is as important as that of who is authorized to have access to or receive information from the system. After a thorough analysis of existing data-gathering procedures, regulations must be devised to establish who is authorized to collect, add to, delete from, or make other changes in the data. They must also specify the conditions under or intervals at which such changes may be made. Controlling data acquisition is the first step toward insuring data base integrity.

PUBLIC AND RESTRICTED RECORDS

Some data are legally defined as "public records," which must be made available to any person who wishes to see them. The assessed valuation of real property and the city's official budgets are usually so defined by state law. Other data may not be defined by law as public records, but in the absence of any demonstration that the data are sensitive, they should be made available to anyone who wishes to see them, subject only to questions of cost and convenience.

On the other hand, by state law the release of certain data may be restricted to specified individuals. In some states, for example, copies of a birth certificate may be issued only to the person to whom the record of birth relates, if of age, or to a parent or other lawful representative. Similarly, access to adoption records and juvenile court records is usually severely restricted by state statute.

However, much of the data that a municipality may have in its information system will not be specifically defined by statute as either public records or of limited access, and judgments have to be made about who may receive them. Hence the analysis of the data should be geared toward determining whether or not particular items should be restricted to a particular level of access, as a condition of integrating them with other data in the data base.

Some data, such as police intelligence information, may need to be restricted to a few individuals in a single city agency and kept entirely from all others, including the public. Indeed, it may be decided that it would be best if such data were not put into the integrated data base at all.

CLASSES OF SENSITIVITY

Items of data are always available to someone, but not necessarily to everyone. In simplistic terms, either an item is available to all persons, public and governmental, or access to it is restricted to specifically authorized recipients only. However, these two classifications, "open" and "restricted," are overly broad. In order to protect both the public's right to know and the individual's right to privacy, the restricted category should be broken down into as many different types as the sensitivity of data contained in the system may warrant.

As has been discussed earlier, an inventory and analysis of all the data to be maintained in the municipal information system is a key step in determining who shall be authorized to have access to particular data. This analysis should include a determination of the level of sensitivity of each type of data.

Since the development of an integrated municipal information system requires that all data elements be identified and described, both by their source and by the uses to which they are put, the determination of the level of sensitivity of the data elements can be made at the same time. Indeed, the source of the data and the uses to which they are put are important factors in determining who shall have access to them.

SENSITIVITY TRANSIENCE

Some data may be sensitive at a particular time but lose the need for confidentiality at a later date; for example, an analysis of alternatives for purchases of real property or of bid limits for city purchases needs to be kept confidential before the announcement of the specific purchases or opening bids, but once the purchase has been made the need for confidentiality no longer exists.

DATA ENVIRONMENT AND SENSITIVITY

The environment in which the data are stored or maintained can have an effect on the sensitivity of the data. A small, uncoordinated manual file may have little sensitivity; yet when it is placed into the environment of an integrated information system these data, in combination with other, equally accessible data, may acquire a sensitivity and need for confidentiality that is not intrinsic to the individual items.

Hence, data must be evaluated and classified not only by their inherent sensitivity but also considering those data in combination with the other data residing in the data base. While some of these decisions can be made beforehand and reflected in regulations, it will often not be possible to do so until such time as a request is made for combinations of data; in such a case the wisdom of releasing them must be decided when the request is made.

DEDICATED SYSTEMS

One of the major debates in American government today deals with the way police data of various sorts should be controlled. One school of thought insists that all police data should be maintained in "dedicated" computer systems, which are systems for the exclusive use of, and under the control of, law enforcement agencies. It is argued that this is justified by their extraordinary requirements for security of the data base.

Opponents of dedicated systems reject this argument, pointing out that there are enough hardware and software techniques available to assure the protection of police data. Furthermore, they argue, (1) most cities cannot afford to maintain two separate computer facilities; (2) maintenance of a separate information system by the police reduces management control by elected officials over a vital area of municipal government; (3) since much of the data in a police information system is not sensitive, the benefits of the data sharing possible in an integrated system would be lost to both the police and all others; and (4) the maintenance of a dedicated police information system responsible to no one represents a very real threat to civil liberties.

ACCURACY OF DATA

Concern for both privacy and the effectiveness of the system requires that the data maintained in an information system be accurate and complete; yet it must be recognized that any system involving thousands of records cannot be totally free from error. Therefore, reasonable efforts to identify and correct the inaccuracies that are bound to occur must be made on a continuing and systematic basis. This is particularly true when the data may be of a sensitive nature.

Each agency that generates data that enters the system must be required to conduct periodic audits to ensure that the operating files are regularly and accurately updated. Incomplete or stale information can be as damaging as erroneous information. When errors or incompleteness are detected, there is of course an obligation to repair the record immediately.

One technique that increases confidence in a data base is that of including the citizen in the auditing process. For some categories of records, for example those that include personal information, it is wise to send a copy to the person to whom the record relates for purposes of verification. Where there is no return, the record can be assumed to be correct. Where the respondent does challenge the accuracy or completeness of the record, routine procedures should be devised for responding to the challenge and for making the corrections that may result. This is done to a considerable extent even now, as in the case of municipal utility bills and tax bills.

There is a less widely recognized, but equally important, obligation to inform everyone who has recieved a copy of a faulty record, file, or listing that the previous information was in error and should be disregarded and the correct information substituted. This requires that a log or register be maintained of all recipients of data from the system, so that follow-ups can be made if necessary. Regulations should be devised that explicitly reflect these requirements.

ELIMINATION OF DATA

Closely allied to the problem of verification of the accuracy of data maintained in the system is the question of elimination of data. Procedures must be established for determining when, and under what circumstances, data is to be purged from the system.

Each data element and file should be examined to determine whether it has a finite life span. Provision should be made for expunging certain data or files whenever any of the following conditions exist:

- They are no longer useful because the purpose for which they were collected has been satisfied.
- They are obsolete because their age makes them unreliable for present purposes.
- There is no longer a legitimate need for maintaining the information in active files.

It may be that some data or files may no longer be useful for current purposes but may have historical or analytical value. In such cases, provision should be made for removing them from active files and retiring them to storage.

ACCESS TO DATA

The policies, regulations, and operating procedures governing access to data are at the heart of any information system concerned with the protection of individual privacy and data confidentiality. While there are threats to the system from outsiders—people not authorized to have access to the system—it is in some respects easier to insure the security of an automated information system than it is to secure manual files.

The greater threat comes from people who are authorized to have access to the system's data and who may deliberately or inadvertently abuse their right to access. It is essential that regulations be created that make explicit who the authorized users of the system are, what data may be released to each user, when and how often the data may be released to each user, and at what level of detail or aggregation they should be released in each case. The regulations should also place restrictions on the disclosure of the data by authorized users to unauthorized persons and provide penalties for infractions of the regulations.

Maintaining a record of who has had access, or attempted to have access, to particular data, and for what purpose, is essential to an effective audit of the users of the system. In most instances the keeping of this audit trail can be automated.

It is also a common practice, as when users are operating from a remote terminal, to automate the system's refusal to yield data to an authorized user who makes an unauthorized inquiry. In such instances a "flag is raised" in data processing, so that the data access control supervisor may be notified.

The "Need to Know" Test

One guideline frequently used by governments in determining whether or not a user should have access to particular information is the "need to know" the information. This guideline may be useful in the administration of a municipal information system, since experience has demonstrated that there are criteria for determining when someone needs to know something. Routinely applied, this guideline can stop inquiries about sensitive data based on mere curiosity.

Useful though the "need to know" guideline is, however, it cannot automatically establish the legitimacy of "need to know" claims, although it can, in the light of existing policies, regulations, and operating procedures, provide a common-sense guideline for administrators of the system to use.

It should be emphasized that this test is only useful in the case of requests for information generated within the administration and has no application to requests for information that are generated by citizens or private organizations. In the interest of keeping the operations of government visible to the public, no request for information from the private sector should be denied on the basis of the "need to know" rule.

Simple Aggregation

Operators, managers, and planners in the city administration and researchers, market analyzers, realtors, and others from the private sector are more often interested in aggregations of data, or statistical summaries, than in listings of individual records. In this instance the users are more interested in the activities of groupings of individuals than in the activities of single individuals.

Aggregated data of this type pose no threat of compromise to individual privacy where the number of records aggregated is sufficiently large, even though the particular data elements on the aggregated records may be sensitive. The Census Bureau and the Social Security Administration have successfully protected the confidentiality of individual records for many years, while making much data available to the public and to other governmental agencies in the form of statistical summaries.

Discretion will be necessary, however, in determining whether or not the number of records aggregated is large enough to protect the anonymity of those to whom the individual records relate. To take an extreme example, it should be obvious that aggregating the data on only two records and reporting a statistical summary of averages of the personal incomes of dwellers in a particular sector of the city, say a block face, permits more than a guess as to who makes what. Again, the application of common sense should be sufficient in arriving at a good decision about any request for aggregated data.

Complex Aggregations

Requests for aggregated data will often come with the requirement that the user be able to perform correlations between the data elements. For example, if I desired to know how many persons owning real property in the city do not live in the city, I would have to examine parcel data in order to establish the names of owners and municipal census data in order to establish the names of city residents. A correlation of the two listings would then reveal the desired information. This means that I would have to be able to look at individual, nonaggregated records in order to get the final tally I desire.

Nevertheless, requests for this type of data need not be refused as a threat to individual privacy if certain precautions are taken. The records can be supplied with all identifying information, such as name, address, social security number, driver's license number, and employee number, stripped away and an arbitrarily assigned serial number affixed to records relating to the same individual in each file. The user may be supplied the two listings of records, but may correlate them by reference to the serial numbers on each list.

A word of caution, however: Where the number of data elements is very large and the number of records is very small, the anonymity of each record in the file becomes threatened. In such cases the request for data should be refused. To illustrate, we have all had the experience of trying to identify an individual whose name we can't recall, to someone else. The process goes like this: (1) his nickname is Doc; (2) he lives on Elm Street; (3) he drives a Chevy; (4) he works in a grocery store; (5) he is about 40 years old; and so on. At some point the person we are talking to will have sufficient identifying information, if he in fact knows the person, to single out the individual from a fairly large number of acquaintances. The chances of recognition are increased with each variable for which data is supplied, as in (1) through (5) above. The same technique applies in identifying individuals from correlatable data; thoughtful judgment will be required in deciding whether requests for this kind of data can be satisfied.

SALE OF DATA

In many instances governmental agencies have sold data pertaining to individuals to private commercial interests. It is a common practice of state motor vehicle departments to sell auto registration and driver's license information. As cities automate their information systems and data is more readily and economically accessible, there may well be pressure experienced by them to sell public record data.

The question of prohibiting the bulk sales of identifiable personal data will have to be decided. Needless to say, this can become a stormy issue, since many people object to becoming targets of sales personnel because of the fact that information that they have been required to give to government agencies has been used for purposes other than that for which it was collected. It should be determined what data, if any, should be sold for commercial purposes. If personal data is to be sold, it may be that citizens should be given an opportunity to have their names deleted from the list that is made available for commercial purposes. This process can be automated.

SYSTEM FLEXIBILITY

Although it must be clearly understood who may have access to what data, the regulations should be so restrictive as to preclude legitimate but unanticipated uses of data. Since all contingencies cannot be anticipated before the system becomes operational, it is essential that procedures be devised by which data can be released for new routine applications or for granting ad hoc requests for data.

It should be kept in mind that the creation of an integrated data base opens up the possibility of many new uses of data, both within the city administration and by private citizens or groups of citizens. It should be anticipated that the growth curve of data requests will probably climb steeply as the capabilities of the system become known.

The reasons for this anticipated growth are three: (1) data is accessible in a much shorter time and with greater economy than before; (2) the user is not restricted to a single record but may draw data from a variety of records that are otherwise unrelated and may have originated in more than one department, since the data are sharable between all departments of the city administration; and (3) there now exists an explicit listing, or inventory, of all of the data collected by the city, making it possible, for example, for a department head to scan the list of available data for additional data that will improve the performance of his department.

This new availability of data will also generate substantial numbers of requests for data from other sectors, such as from realtors and colleges, for research in a variety of fields. There will be requests for selective mailing lists, such as lists of real property owners, payers of city income taxes, renters, and many others.

Each of these requests generates questions about propriety and costs, questions that are not easily resolved, although a system of procedures has been instituted for dealing with them. Even with procedures, the dividing point between the competing principles of right to know and right to privacy is not easily established by a general rule, but must be resolved on an individual basis. In any event, the system must be flexible enough to respond to all of these situations in a manner that is economically feasible.

You will note that the solution we have offered in the discussion of each problem area has been the same, namely the institution of a system of routine procedures. These procedures will be discussed in Chapters 8 and 9, and models provided. Before we reach that point there are two problem areas yet to be discussed: auditing and physical security.

FURTHER REFERENCES

For additional information with respect to special problem areas of data access control, we particularly recommend Privacy and Computers (Ottawa: Information Canada, 1972), a report prepared by a Canadian Task Force established jointly by the Departments of Communications and Justice, and Records, Computers and the Rights of Citizens (Washington: U.S. Government Printing Office, 1973), a report prepared by the Advisory Committee on Automated Personal Data Systems, for the Secretary of the U.S. Department of Health, Education and Welfare.

NOTES

1. See Tables 2, 3, and 4 in Chapter 4.
2. See Note 6 in Chapter 1.

6

AUDITING DATA
PROCESSING OPERATIONS

Many cities have obtained computers to replace the calculating equipment used by finance department bookkeepers. However, this change of equipment has introduced a profound difference in the way finance departments have operated from that time forward. Instead of dealing only with bookkeepers and internal auditing controls, the finance departments had now also to deal with data processing personnel and the mysteries of what they were doing.

The internal auditing controls that had existed before continued to exist, but now with a large gap produced between the input to data processing and the output received from it. This data processing gap in auditing controls is critical in view of the potential for either mischief or undetected error.

The purpose of this chapter is to examine the varieties of error and mischief and to suggest some methods of control by which they may be reduced and perhaps avoided altogether; but first it is necessary that the reader have at least a minimal understanding of how software is generated.

THE DEVELOPMENT OF SOFTWARE

One of the largest single investments a city makes to a data processing capability is in the initial generation of software and thereafter in its maintenance and augmentation. We are able to communicate with a computer only by the use of a few very limited, stylized languages such as FORTRAN, COBOL, and PL/I. Once one language is learned, the others are learned quickly. The vocabularies of these languages are very limited, but the variations in the use of the vocabularies are numerous, thus giving considerable flexibility in the kinds of instructions we give to the computer.

Much as we employ interpreters when communicating with people who speak another language, we employ programmers to communicate our instructions to the computer. A finance director, for example, will supply a narrative of what he desires, and the programmer will translate the narrative into a computer language. In finance, COBOL is probably the language most often used, even though an assembly language may be more efficient.

An intermediate person is needed to complete the linkage between the finance director and the computer. A programmer very often has only the skill to interpret program specifications into the codes required for the computer; that is to say, he must be provided with a listing of the input data elements, a flow chart of how they are to be processed, and a formatted listing of the data elements that are the output of that processing. By "format," we mean the sequence in which the output fields are to be printed and the definition of those fields, that is, their length. This may entail either the design of a new form or accommodation to an existing old one. Examples would include the format of a check, of a statement, or of various listings of data.

The person who completes the link between the finance director and the programmer is an analyst; programmers who have both analytic and programming skills are called programmer-analysts. The analyst guides the interview with the finance director and with others he may have to consult and rearranges the narrative thus produced to define a system, still in narrative form. He then supplements the narrative with a flow chart, which indicates the descriptive names of the input data, its sources, the manner in which it is to be processed, the output that is desired, and the arrangement of that output. He also provides special instructions in narrative form about frequency of processing, storage and retirement of both input and output files, data access control restrictions, and delivery of output documents.

The interview usually proceeds from a careful definition of what is desired as an output document. A study is then made of the input data that will be necessary to produce the output document and of the sources of that input data. Where all of the kinds of data required are not at that time routinely produced in the system, the analyst must make provisions for its production. In some instances this may prove impractical, in which cases the interview resumes in an effort to assess the effect on the desired output document of the compromises that this makes necessary.

The process is iterative, in the sense that the analyst may have to retrace his interviewing steps many times, perhaps enlarging the circle of persons and offices consulted in the process. The process is also iterative over a longer time. Circumstances may change, making changes in the output document desirable. The analyst is therefore concerned not only with the original design of an application, but also with its review over a period of years to ensure its continuing usefulness.

These procedures ultimately result in a program design or specification of the application that is desired, for example an accounts payable application. The programmer codes from this specification in the programming language and produces a source program. The source program is run on the computer through a manufacturer-supplied program called a compiler. This translates the source program into what is known as machine language, the language a computer recognizes. In addition, the compiler verifies the correctness of the use of the programming language itself; that is to say, it examines the program for syntactical errors. If there is a fault in the source program, the computer will refuse to compile the program but will instead generate what are known as the diagnostics, a listing of the errors the compiler has found.

When these errors are corrected and the source program is successfully compiled, there still remains another kind of test, which relates to the ability of the program to produce a correct output from a given input. A test deck of input data is prepared in which the correct output has been independently computed; this test deck should be designed to exercise each of the contingencies the program is designed to meet. This in itself can be a difficult and lengthy task. When the test has been met and the machine operator supplied with operating instructions, then presumably the application is ready to become operational, at least within the data processing center.

The program and processes, however detailed, precise, and systematic their development to this point may have been, are still almost assured of error, unintentional or deliberate. In the sections to follow we will consider some of the errors and what can be done to reduce them.

TARGETS OF CONTROL

Error, whether deliberate or unintentional, may result from two sources: (1) changes in the input data itself, such as from careless conversion of hard copy data into machine-readable media, for example in keypunching an input document, and (2) unauthorized changes in the software, that is, in the programs that tell the computer how to process the data it receives.

Keypunching

The first and most obvious source of error is keypunching or
whatever other method translates the hard copy source document into
machine-readable media. The opportunities for keypunching error
are at least as great as those in using an ordinary typewriter. Since
figures that ultimately will be assessed in dollars predominate, the
impact of errors can be substantial. For this reason a verifying
machine must always be used as a companion to the keypuncher.
Furthermore, the same operator should not be employed to verify
data that he himself has keypunched. When errors are discovered,
the hard copy input document should be reintroduced at the beginning
of the keypunch-verify cycle. When it has been keypunched correctly
it should be reinserted in its position in the machine-readable file.

The effect of this procedure is to minimize the opportunity not
only for casual error but also for deliberate error, since deliberate
error can only result from the collusion of the keypuncher and the
verifier. If the shop is large enough to employ more than one keypuncher and verifier they should not be used as teams, but rather
associated on a random basis as directed by the supervisor, thus
reducing the possibility of collusion.

A further check of the correctness of the data can be built into
the programs that will process the data; these are known as reasonableness checks, about which more will be said below.

We spoke of collusion—collusion about what? The possibilities
are as varied as imagination permits. The most obvious relate to
the keypunching of payroll and accounts payable information. Increases in hours worked, in rates of pay, in amounts of supplies
ordered and hence amounts to be paid to a supplier—all of these
merely scratch the surface. It will be immediately argued that these
would be caught in a manual audit; but how often are audits conducted,
given the lengths of the listings? What periods of time are covered
in the audits? How large a sample is obtained? And finally, is the
computer itself employed in the conduct of the audits?

Programs

The second source of error, whether deliberate or unintentional,
is the program that processes a particular set of data. To understand how a program can be used as a source both of data correction
and of data error, it is necessary to understand something of the
nature of programming.

A program is a listing of sequentially numbered statements.
Each statement represents an instruction to the computer that is
roughly equivalent to the following segment of a program (in which
liberties have been taken for purposes of simplification):

Statement Number	Instruction
10	Read the input data, employee number, name, hours worked, rate per hour
20	For each, multiply hours worked by rate, equals pay
30	For each, print the input data together with pay

One of the kinds of statements typically used at various points in the program is an "if, then" statement. This statement enables a programmer to direct that "if" a certain circumstance exists, "then, go to" a particular numbered statement for the next instruction. This particular numbered statement typically will be out of the regular processing sequence, representing a special circumstance. This device is useful in many ways, but here we are concerned with its use both as a means of testing the correctness of input data and as a means of introducing error into input data. An example is provided in the following section.

Tests of Reasonableness and of Logic

By testing the reasonableness of input data, we compare the input data with its logical limits. For example, if we prepare a listing of job codes, together with the lowest and highest hourly wages possible for each job code, and if we also input the job code of each employee when the application program is run, we can instruct the computer to alert us if the hourly wage of a particular employee does not fall within the range specified for his job code. The following will illustrate (again taking liberties with the syntax of computer programs for purposes of simplification):

Statement Number	Instruction
100	Read the input data, job code, hourly wage
110	If hourly wage is less than or more than that specified in look-up table then go to 200
• • •	[other statements]
200	Print operator message: error in input data, employee number, hourly wage, job code
210	Go to 100

46

In the above example we chose to have a message printed to the machine operator each time an error was discovered and then to return to the processing of the remaining input data. This would result in a listing of errors that would accompany the output of the program when it was delivered to the finance department. Corrective action could then be taken. Note that we could have instructed the computer to print the error message and then to interrupt processing until such time as the input error was corrected. Circumstances will dictate which method is to be preferred; that is to say, whether or not processing is to be interrupted.

It will not always be possible to specify a look-up table with reference to existing ranges of data, as in the foregoing example. However, such tables can be created by simple exercises in logic. Hours worked, for example, cannot exceed 168 per week, assuming the employee is on the job 24 hours per day for seven days; but this is a poor assumption. We would like to test hours worked per week with reference to the usual pattern and to be informed by an "error listing" or "exception listing" about any employee not falling within that pattern. We may arbitrarily decide that we want a separate listing of all employees who were inputted as having worked any overtime at all and, additionally, an asterisk for any employee credited with more than, say, eight hours overtime per week.

It is through this kind of flexibility in computer-tested input data that we are able to reduce error. Reasonableness, or logical tests, can be built into applications programs to test virtually every inputted data element. In the aggregate these tests cause the operating time, and hence the expense, of data processing to increase; but the alternative is to accept the risk of a higher incidence of error, which can be much more expensive.

The creation of these tests call for close study, imagination, and at times innovation. It is a time-consuming process that represents considerable additional effort for analysts and programmers. For this reason it is unlikely that the programs will contain reasonableness tests unless the analysts and programmers are instructed to incorporate them on a routine basis in the designs of their programs.

Deliberate Program Errors

By deliberate program errors, we mean the insertion of un-authorized statements into a program for the purpose of creating error in the output. The risk of discovery of unauthorized statements in a program is slight in the typical data processing center of a typical city, for three reasons.

First, the average program contains hundreds of lines of state-ments and comments, and the unauthorized statements may be "buried" in their midst.

Second, since the statements are in an esoteric language they would not be recognized by laymen, such as auditors trained in finance but not in EDP.

Third, while the source deck listing, and sometimes the source deck itself, sets forth statements in a form that approaches plain language, the compiled deck does not, and it is the compiled deck that a machine operator uses after the first run.* This means that the machine operator does not see a readable program listing even if he knows how to program. In small shops the source deck is usually returned to the programmer-analyst after the first run. The programmer-analyst retains custody of it for such purposes as program maintenance from that time forward.

All of this means that unless there is a periodic audit of its software by someone who is knowledgeable in programming and data processing, the average city is vulnerable to fraud and embezzlement originating in the data processing department.

To provide one example, assume that I, as a programmer, am in collusion with John Doe. Assume further that in the portion of the payroll application program having to deal with reading the input (machine-readable) file, specifically employee number and rate of pay, I insert a statement that instructs that "if" John Doe's employee number is read, "then" increase his indicated hourly wage by, say, 25 percent.

In a similar manner the quantity or cost of merchandise can be altered during an accounts payable application by a data processing employee in collusion with a firm with which the city does business.

A somewhat different kind of deliberate error that is accomplished with unauthorized program statements involves an instruction to produce a check to a specified, but fictitious, employee or vendor each time the program is run. The chances are that none of these crimes would be discovered except by an audit of the software.

But it should be remembered that an audit of the software involves more than reading the program listings. This alone would not be sufficient because unauthorized statements can be suppressed on a listing of the program. It involves, more importantly, a run with actual data for a prior period, and the results compared with the results of independent processing of the same data. Even this precaution could be defeated where the offender has had access to the compiled program and has been able to substitute a "clean" program, as in instances where notice of the pending audit is given.

---

*Note that, increasingly, object programs are stored directly on peripherals, for example disks, from the compilation and are called upon when needed. Thus the operator may never see the program listing.

The range of conventional internal and external post-audit techniques, as for a manual operation, continue to apply, but with the addition of electronic data processing they simply do not go far enough. The foregoing examples merely scratch the surface of the potential for this kind of mischief. The possibilities are limited only by the imagination and criminality of the offender, together with laxity, or even absence of controls, in the department in which the offender is employed.

FURTHER REFERENCES

For additional information with respect to software security we particularly recommend two books, Jancura's Computers: Auditing and Control (Philadelphia: Auerbach, 1973) and Van Tassel's Computer Security Management (Englewood Cliffs, N.J.: Prentice-Hall, 1972). Jancura ensures a diversity of viewpoints with respect, for example, to "The Accountant's Role in the Computer Revolution," by a wide selection of authors for the many articles the book contains. Van Tassel is particularly valuable for his discussions of fraud and data processing insurance and for the check-off lists he provides for significant areas of vulnerability.

7

PHYSICAL
SECURITY OF THE DATA
PROCESSING SYSTEM

Questions of confidentiality and privacy are resolved in a legal, political, and social context. Questions of security, on the other hand, are resolved in an economic context: security costs money. Therefore, important determinations to be made are: (1) the value of the thing to be protected; (2) the risk we are willing to assume; and (3) how much we are willing to invest in the cost of protection.

The value of the data processing center and peripheral equipment is really composed of two quite different parts. The obvious part is physical equipment; the not so obvious part is the cost of restoring files. In many instances, particularly in the case of historical records, the importance of the data can be greater than the value of the physical plant.

PROTECTION OF FILES

The cost of restoring data will vary according to procedures followed by the data processing center: Three examples follow: (1) A well organized system will retire successive generations of data in either punch card or magnetic tape reels to a completely separate, well protected location. (2) For added protection, successive generations of manual files from which the data was gathered will be returned to an entirely different, well protected location. (3) A poorly organized center may merely retire manual records and the latest machine-readable update to a storage room within the center.

The result in the first two instances is that only current files, the files presently being processed, will be present in the computer center at any time. Should the files at the center be destroyed, it would merely be necessary to update the last generation of the files stored in a remote location. Should these, too, be destroyed it would be necessary to restore the machine-readable files from the manual files (hard copy records), also remotely stored.

It should be obvious that the cost of restoring files in the first instance would be relatively little; in the second instance it would be relatively more; but in the third instance, wherein local storage procedures for all files were employed, it would not be to restore the files.

It is useful to think of successive generations of files in terms of "son," "father," "grandfather," "great-grandfather," and so on. These constitute historical records, whether in manual file storage or in machine-readable storage. Since these files rapidly accumulate in most installations, it will be necessary to address questions of file retirement. In formulating policies of file retirement it will be necessary to set policies governing the retirement of manual files as distinguished from those that are machine-readable. Policies may be expressed in terms of time, for example, "retain for one year," but in many instances it will be more convenient to express such policies in terms of the number of generations. As a "son" is added, in this parlance, a "great-grandfather" is retired. The policy may require the retirement of a particular generation of a manual file into the medium of microfilm and, following this, the destruction of the manual file.

Estimates of the cost of restoring files in the first two examples are not difficult to calculate. The first instance involves the cost of conversion of the manual records for transactions in the last period and of processing the most recently retired historical file through an update procedure. This same calculation must be made for each file requiring an update. The sum of all of this, together with operating time, constitutes the estimate. This estimate should be compared with the cost of restoration in the second instance; this comparison should be considered in determining the method to be used.

Estimates of the cost of restoring files in the second example will be based upon the conversion of not only the current data, but also the conversion of the last generation of historical manual files into machine-readable form. Keep in mind that conversion cost, for example keypunching, can be the greatest single expense of data processing, expressed in dollars, time, and the results of errors.

The difference in estimates, then, represents the base against which the added cost of separate storage facilities and procedures will be compared. An assumption will also have to be made about the frequency at which file restoration will be required. This will be a function, to some extent, of the measure of protection afforded the data processing installations.

The custodian of retired files, whether manual or machine-readable, should not be the data processing chief or any of his employees. This is true for the same reason that good accounting procedures advise against the consolidation of accounts payable and accounts receivable. The opportunities for abuse are too obvious to require additional elaboration.

Historical files should be placed in a fireproof, secure location. As the oldest generation of manual files are converted to microfilm, these should be placed in yet another secure location: ideally, a fireproof safe.

Historical machine-readable files should be identified by adequate documentation. If catalogue or file numbers are used, the documentation explaining the identification of the file by number should also be stored, but in still a different location, to ensure that the custodian of historical files will not be able to describe the contents of any particular file. The file can only be issued by reference to its file number.

While these procedures would seem to involve the assignment of too many persons to the various duties, it should be kept in mind that for the most part we are speaking of file custodians. This cannot be thought of as a full-time job in most cities, but rather as a collateral duty of persons presently employed in some other primary role, such as in the city clerk's office or the finance department.

PROTECTION OF SOFTWARE

So far we have spoken about the protection of data files. There is yet another, equally important category of "data" that requires similar protection in the interest of establishing audit trails and restoration capability, and that is the software, the programs that tell the computer how to process the data.

An average city employing data processing is probably investing a significant portion of its data processing personnel cost in program development and maintenance. By program development, we mean the design, the development of program specifications, the flow-charting, and the coding (that is, programming). By maintenance we mean progressive improvement in the program by revisions resulting in greater efficiencies, correction of mistakes, or changes in response to changes in the system.

Software, that is to say the machine-readable instructions, is accompanied by documentation in hard copy files, including a listing of the statements in the program, explanatory comments where desirable, flow charts, program specifications, documents relating it to other programs, a listing of the data files required and the sources of those files, provisions for data access control requirements, and any other information that may contribute to a full understanding of the program.

Software and software documentation require the same measures of protection that are accorded the data files of which we have been speaking. Furthermore, since programs may go through a number of revisions, we again have generations of programs. In program documentation it is essential that changes in the program be dated. Again, this is to assure an auditable trail of the historical use of those programs.

The destruction, accidentally or deliberately, of software files and software documentation inevitably results in a great restoration expense. It is therefore important that a duplicate of the machine-readable programs be stored in a separate secure location, since the duplication of programs is fast and relatively inexpensive. It is equally important that successive editions of the same programs be similarly stored. All of these might, for example, be stored in the machine-readable data files location.

Paralleling the storage of software, copies of software documentation and changes in software documentation should be stored in a different secure location. Again, the storage facility used for hard copy files should do.

What has been described up to this point are methods that ensure the ability to restore files of data and software while at the same time retaining a historical record that is sufficient to permit all transactions during the period to be audited. You will recall that data processing abuses can be perpetrated as much by unauthorized changes in programs as by alteration of data files.

PROTECTION OF EQUIPMENT: INSURANCE

At the start of this chapter we spoke of the value of the things to be protected. So far we have discussed only the data and program files, and we have found the costs to be primarily those of file duplication and the maintenance of two fireproof, secure storage facilities. These are tangible costs and may be estimated.

As for the hardware and peripherals—such as the computer or central processing unit, the lister or printer, the various direct access memory units, the tape drives, the card readers; the communications equipment; and the terminals, such as CRT (cathode ray tube) or teletype—the more conventional means of protection, at least in an economic sense, are by insurance.

Decisions with respect to insurance will depend upon whether the city owns, leases, or rents the equipment. The city should not assume that rented equipment is adequately insured by the owner. The rental contract should be studied and a decision made about whether or not there is sufficient protection against liability.

Furthermore, the inventory of data storage media such as tapes and punch cards should be considered as a candidate for insurance if the value is very great. To this should be added an estimate of restoration cost, which is also insurable. Finally, to this total should be added an estimate of the cost of interim equipment rentals, so as to ensure continuation of data processing activities without unacceptable interruption.

Premiums on insurance will vary substantially according to the vulnerability of the installation to fire, theft, or other hazards. In this sense an insurance examination or inspection is useful for the indices of security in the checkoff list it provides and for the expert evaluation of risks.

PHYSICAL HAZARDS

Physical hazards to the data processing center are created by the threats of fire, water, air-conditioning failure, power failure, disaster, penetration by unauthorized persons, and sabotage from within.

Fire

The fire protection considerations of a data processing center are not greatly different from those of other offices or installations except in two respects: (1) the mass of electric power cables and electronic machinery poses particular problems when water is used to put out a blaze and (2) the high density capital investment of the center itself makes a higher level of protection desirable.

Insurance inspectors, fire department personnel, and fire prevention equipment vendors are excellent sources of advice about the needed level of protection and, equally important, all provide periodic follow-up inspection services. However, there certain obvious and important considerations can be stated at this point.

The data processing center should be located in a fireproof building, or failing that should be located in an area of the building constructed of fireproof materials, in which heat and smoke sensors and alarms have been located on each wall, the ceiling, and the floor. The center should be partitioned with fireproof materials into work spaces, so that if a fire occurs in one space it can be contained before reaching another. The tons of paper rolling through the line printers, and overflowing waste baskets, constitute distinct fire hazards. Each space should utilize only fireproofed furniture.

Each room should be equipped with fire extinguishers, preferably of the nonwater type, and with automatic sprinkler systems in the ceilings. The hand extinguishers should be thought of as the first line of defense against a fire, since damage to electronic equipment and the danger of shorting the electric power cables will be minimized. The master electrical switch should then be pulled in anticipation of the second line of defense, the overhead automatic sprinkler systems, which use water to extinguish the fire. Since it cannot be assured that personnel will always be on hand when the blaze occurs, it is desirable that the sprinkler system be of a type that automatically disengages the power source before activation of the sprinkler. The bibliography should be consulted for sources of additional information about fire threats and protection.

Water

The threat of water has to some extent been discussed with fire protection. However, a greater threat of water damage is from flooding. This may occur from natural causes, and hence the threat must be assessed in terms of the geographic location of the center. If the threat of a flood does exist in the area in which the center is located, it becomes very important to locate the center on a floor of a building that is high enough to minimize the risk—don't select the basement as the location. Further, because of the wind, rain, and flying debris that accompany hurricanes, should the center be located in a region in which hurricanes occur, it becomes particularly important to locate the center in a windowless room. The remaining source of flooding is from the air conditioning unit, in which air is blown over pipes that are cooled by water flowing inside them. The best protection here is to be sure the employees know the location of the cut-off valve for air conditioning each unit.

Air Conditioning Failure

Electronic data processing equipment generates considerable heat. Where this heat is not sufficiently dissipated, machine operating temperatures will exceed design limits, and failure and sometimes permanent damage will occur. Furthermore, malfunction may result from dust and other debris in the air, material that is normally filtered by air conditioning. In some climates humidity will also be a damaging factor, shortening the life of the equipment. For these reasons, data processing centers have received the highest priority in the installation of air conditioning.

While all of these threats are met by satisfactory air conditioning, there are several factors to be considered in deciding upon the kind of air conditioning system to be installed in a data processing center. Reliability will be enhanced if several smaller units are

selected over one large one. Where possible, one unit in excess of
need should be installed on the assumption that one or more units will
be inoperative and under repair from time to time. A second factor
is to ensure that air intake for the units is located away from the
usual sources of dust, sand, or steam. Finally, the wall cavities in
which the units are placed should be protected, to prevent their becoming an avenue of penetration by unauthorized persons.

Power Failure

Computers require a constant voltage at a specified level in
order to function correctly. A power failure may result not only in
a loss of operating capability, but also in a memory purge in the
central processing unit. Brownouts, or voltage reductions, can cause
not only memory purges but also errors in logic.

Unfortunately, the solutions to these contingencies are not
economically justified for most cities; these solutions include independent power sources in the utility network or the installation of
an emergency power supply such as a diesel generator.

However, the city can obtain some measure of protection against
brownout in the data processing shop by installing voltage regulator
transformers. Such transformers maintain the output voltage constant
in spite of variations in the input voltage or may compensate for an
input voltage that is constant but at a level below that specified for
computer operations.

Contingency plans should anticipate an emergency in which
power failure will continue over an extended period. Alternate facilities should be identified in the same city and in nearby cities. The
alternate facilities that are selected should be compatible in terms
of computer language, compiler, and hardware, as far as possible.

Disaster

Cities are vulnerable to a variety of disasters, and they do
occur; witness the number of declared disaster areas per year in
the past. With respect to data processing, it should be assumed that
a disaster will occur, and planning should be directed toward that
contingency.

Planning should include, at the minimum, two primary precautions:
(1) remote storage of machine-readable historical files and software
and of software documentation and (2) prior arrangement for back-up
computer facilities that are also remote from the existing data processing center. This arrangement might take the form of memoranda
of agreement with other cities or with a private business.

Unauthorized Penetration

The data processing facilities of the average city are particularly vulnerable to unauthorized penetration. This is because most cities employ a one or two shift operation, and their centers are rarely in operation on weekends. This leaves many hours per week in which the facility is unguarded, unless other protective steps are taken.

While security technology is a field in which much expertise has been developed, there are a few considerations in matters of security that should be apparent to nonexperts.

Routes of access to the computer center should be limited, hopefully to a single entrance. Doors should be of metal and equipped with a good lock. A method of key discipline should be observed. Interior doors should be utilized to isolate visitor and administrative areas from operations areas. An observing room for visitors, if used at all, should be completely segregated from the rest of the facility while permitting the machine room to be viewed through a Lexon panel. Lexon is a transparent material that can resist the impact of such forces as hammers and even bullets.

Administrative offices, particularly those to which visitors might necessarily be admitted in the ordinary course of business, should be similarly segregated. Visitor logs should be maintained. Visitors to any of the operating units of the facility should be escorted from the visiting room by the person they desire to see, and this escort should be continuous until the visitor has left the premises.

Any of a variety of burglar alarms should be installed and activated for after-hour periods. Hopefully the facility will be windowless, but if it is not, an alarm should be installed for each window and of course each door. Vents should be examined; if they are large enough to admit a person, alarms should be installed for each. Additionally, vents should be screened with a heavy gauge mesh to assure that objects cannot be thrown into the facility.

If the facility is very large, an identification card should be provided for each employee or other person regularly having business in the facility, and these cards should be worn conspicuously. Signs should be posted indicating the areas of limited access and those authorized to unescorted visitors. Also, the employment of closed-circuit television cameras is appropriate in large installations. These can be trained on key areas, such as the entrance and the visitors' room, and monitored at the receptionist's or the security desk.

Hard copy printouts from computer printers and terminals should be locked up in fireproof file cabinets or safes when not in use. A paper shredder should be used for the destruction of hard copy that is no longer needed.

Sabotage from Within

The best guards against sabotage from within are adequate initial screening of employees and periodic screening thereafter. Employees who are disgruntled should be monitored constantly by their supervisor and relieved of duties if their disgruntlement is excessive. An alert supervisor should be sufficiently familiar with his employees and their affairs to recognize disgruntlement or be aware of sabotage motives. Employees should not be permitted to enter the premises after hours except for supervised work. Further, as in large facilities, employees should be limited to access to their own working spaces only. That is to say, programmer-analysts are not permitted in the machine room, and machine room personnel are not permitted in the programming room. Neither should be permitted in the file storage room.

Finally, a comprehensive plan embracing many of the ideas contained in the foregoing material should be prepared and followed. It should provide for periodic and random inspections of the facility to ensure that the plan is being faithfully implemented. In the absence of such inspections physical security will become lax; there will be the illusion of security while in fact the facility will be quite vulnerable.

FURTHER REFERENCE

For additional information with respect to physical security, we particularly recommend the Advanced Management Research Guide to Computer and Software Security (William F. Brown, ed. New York: AMR International, Inc., 1971). This book is of especially great value for the extensive check-off lists it contains and the chapter on contingency planning.

8

At this point the committee members will have reviewed the studies prepared for them, read selected material listed in the bibliography, consulted among themselves, and in general have prepared themselves for making the decisions that together will constitute the draft ordinance on data access control. In this chapter we will provide a discussion of the key features of the ordinance and a model.

The inclusion of all this material would appear to make the task of the committee easy, but this is not so. The committee will probably experience considerable time-consuming disagreement among its members as each decision point is reached. This should not be discouraged, within limits, because it is through this very process that the wider dimensions of the subject will be discovered and the impact of alternatives evaluated in a local context.

Generally, the ordinance should contain the following: (1) general and specific standards of data access, privacy, and security; (2) the stipulation of penalties for violation of the ordinance and/or such regulations as are subsequently drawn within its authority; (3) the creation of an organizational framework consisting, essentially, of a data access control board and a data access control supervisor, charging both with appropriate responsibilities and equipping both with needed resources; and (4) the minimum essential procedural provisions, such as ad hoc requests for data, appeals of administrative decisions, and maintenance of appropriate records.

The remainder of this chapter will deal with each of these provisions by presenting the model ordinance as a sequence of sections, each in turn interrupted by discussion of that particular section before moving to the next.

GENERAL STANDARDS

I. <u>Purpose</u>

The purpose of this ordinance is to create the means by which the following principles may be protected in this jurisdiction:
 A. The right of members of the public to obtain public data and the obligation of the municipal administration to make such data available are affirmed, subject to such exceptions as may be found in law.
 B. The right of individuals to privacy with respect to personal data that is collected by the municipal administration and the obligation of the city to provide reasonable safeguards for the protection of that data against unauthorized divulgence are affirmed, subject to such exceptions as may be found in law.

II. <u>Definitions</u>:

 A. "Public Data" is data relating to the operations, management, and planning of municipal affairs and does not include personal data.
 B. "Personal Data" is data about an individual who may be identified by reference to the data.

It will be noticed that no reference to a computer-based environment has been made in the basic aim of the ordinance. This is because the principles to be protected relate to <u>both</u> the manual and the computer-based modes of the data access control system. The means for providing the required levels of protection will differ in some cases in the two modes in the system, but the principles remain the same.

Furthermore, most cities that use computers will be found to be in a continuing state of conversion from manual to computer-based applications. This conversion process provides an opportunity for rationalization of a city's data-gathering, access, and release policies. New applications normally impinge upon old ones, as when groupings of applications are integrated together, providing an opportunity for the rationalization of the old applications as well as the new.

There will be a temptation to extend the list of definitions to include, at the minimum, the levels of restricted data. To do so would require the committee to arrive prematurely at its decision about how many levels there should be, since the life of the committee will be only about 45 days at this point. There will be time later, while preparing the administrative regulations, to deal with such questions as these.

Finally, both principles refer to "exceptions as may be found in law." We feel that the desire to list those exceptions in each case should be resisted here, unless the exceptions are sufficiently general in nature.

One typical illustration is a state statute requiring that juvenile records be kept restricted, or limited to the view of specified users in the criminal justice system. We feel that this is best dealt with and referenced in an applicable provision of the administrative regulations. The legal study should disclose a number of statutory requirements of this nature.

SPECIFIC STANDARDS

III. Standards of Data Access Control

    A. Data shall not be collected by the city unless it contributes directly to the operations, management, or planning activities of the City in the discharge of the functions for which it is legally responsible.

    B. Data that is collected by the City shall be shared across organizational boundaries, to the extent that there is a manifest need for such sharing.

    C. Personal data shall be protected by such safeguards as may be necessary to ensure that such data is used only for lawful purposes within the City Administration and that it is not made available for any purpose to individuals or groups outside the City Administration, except as provided by law and/or by Section D, below.

    D. Personal data may be made available to individuals or groups outside the City Administration where the data is in an aggregate form and where the number of records in the aggregate is sufficient to protect the anonymity of the individuals to whom the records relate; or where personal identifiers are removed from the listed data.

    E. Data shall be audited periodically to ensure its continued need, correctness and completeness.

    F. The environments in which data are stored or processed shall be inspected periodically to ensure the maintenance of adequate protection against fire and penetration by unauthorized persons.

There will be a temptation to continue the listing of standards beyond those indicated here. We think this temptation should be resisted. To the extent possible, rule making should be left to the realm of the specialized body created to operate the system, the data access control board. There is a natural division, a hierarchical relationship, among principles, standards, and rules.

The existing convention in informal data access control systems is to require a department head to be responsible for the control of the data that department collects. This has resulted in a kind of data provincialism in which one department knows very little about the useful data that can be made available by another department.

In an integrated system, however, control of the data base is centralized, and a department head can no longer exercise direct control over access to his data. This is because he no longer has custody of data other than those that are in the manual files of his department. The data are mainly in the custody of the data processing unit.

The department head may exercise indirect control, however. To accomplish this the convention is adopted that data processing may release no data whatsoever unless it receives an authorization from the department from which the data has originated.

We recommend, however, that this control be assumed by the data access control supervisor, an officer to be discussed at a later point in this chapter. This will in fact promote the explication of the data base, that is, the publishing of a data dictionary to all departments, and this will promote a demand for greater interdepartmental data sharing. Thus, centralized control of data access will be required. Even so, a data access control supervisor must consult with the department heads involved in a data sharing transaction in order to be advised of all of the implications of the transaction before making a decision with respect to it.

The provision with respect to the release of personal data is highly controversial. As written, the city would not be allowed to release selected mailing lists, advise insurance companies of individual moving-traffic violations, or release other personal data for which there is demand. Yet this is not an uncommon practice among states as well as cities. The decision to include this provision or to qualify it by inserting "except with the approval of the data access control board," can only be made in local context.

The provision with respect to the release of data in aggregate form will of course require the judgment of the data access control board about whether the anonymity of individuals is sufficiently protected in the aggregate.

The next two provisions, relating to the conduct of periodic audits of data and periodic inspections of storage and processing points in the system, may be omitted, since both are identified as tasks of the data access control board and supervisor. We have included them only for purposes of reinforcement of their importance.

IV. Penalties for Noncompliance

   A. Employees of the City Administration who willfully or through
      neglect violate any of the provisions of Section III, Standards
      of Data Access Control, of this ordinance, shall be subject
      to one or both of the following penalties, as may be appro-
      priate:

   1. Personnel action resulting in suspension or dismissal.
   2. Upon conviction, being deemed guilty of a misdemeanor and
   subject to a fine of not more than _____ dollars, _____ months
   imprisonment, or both.

   B. Each instance of unauthorized collection, use, or disclosure
      of personal data shall constitute a separate offense.
   The foregoing model assumes that cities are adequately equipped
with ordinances with respect to crimes such as trespass, burglary,
theft, and embezzlement and that all that is additionally required are
provisions relating to misconduct in office by municipal employees.
With respect to these latter, this provision of the model ordinance
will take a different form according to whether or not there is a
municipal civil service system. If there is, penalties for misconduct
in office may already be specified, at least to the extent of personnel
actions.
   It is significant that only one of the example cities, Dayton,
Ohio, has an ordinance providing criminal penalties for unauthorized
disclosure of information. This ordinance is a part of the Dayton
Income Tax Ordinance, and stipulates that all information received
by the Division of Taxation is confidential; thus the "unauthorized
disclosure" relates only to income tax information. A useful example
of the means by which the superintendent of the Division of Taxation
communicates these provisions to each employee of the division is
set forth in Appendix C.
   In contrast, neither the Wichita Falls nor the Charlotte ordinances provide criminal penalties for unauthorized disclosure. It is
our view that both personnel action and criminal penalties should be
available for enforcement of the ordinance. This ensures the availability of a wider number of options to the city, and hence the selection
of penalties most appropriate for each violation.

THE DATA ACCESS CONTROL BOARD

V. <u>Creation of a Data Access Control Board</u>

    A. There is hereby created a Data Access Control Board to be composed of the following members:

Ex Officio Members: City Manager, as Board Chairman; three department heads of the City Administration, to be appointed by the City Manager; Data Access Control Supervisor, as non-voting Board Secretary; City Attorney, as nonvoting advisor

<u>Members:</u> three private citizens of this city, by appointment by the Mayor, confirmed by the city council.

    B. The term of appointment is for two years, and private citizens appointed to the Board shall serve without pay. Vacancies shall be filled by the appointing authority. The Board shall meet at such regular intervals as are determined by the Board and at other times at the call of the Chairman.

VI. <u>Staff support for the board</u>

    A. Technical and clerical support shall be provided to the Board by the Office of the Data Access Control Supervisor. (See Section VIII, below.)

Experience with three particular cities that have formed data access control boards indicates that wide choices are possible with respect to the composition of the board. Long Beach, California, for example, chose to contain the responsibilities for data access control fully within the administration, that is, in the city manager's office. In Wichita Falls, Texas, all members were private citizens. In Charlotte, North Carolina, most of the members were private citizens, in contrast to the composition we have recommended. Unfortunately, the boards in the example cities have not functioned for enough time to permit comparative evaluation and the determination of the best composition.

We justify our recommendation in part on the merit of diversity in membership and in part on "executive edge." Diversity in membership makes it more probable that the administration will be well informed and advised with respect to the comparative benefits and costs of the alternative solutions under consideration. Executive edge, which means the loading of the board with an imbalance between public officers and private citizens and the assigning of the city manager to the chairmanship of the committee, is in simple recognition of the fact that the administration will be responsible for carrying out the mandates of the board; it therefore seems important that the mandates be digestible to the city manager. As chairman, he will be in a position to exert greater influence on the outcome of the board's decisions.

The example cities vary also in the number of members assigned to the board: Charlotte appointed seven; Wichita Falls, five. While diversity of viewpoints is best assured by a large membership, larger memberships also make it more difficult to get business done, to reach decisions. Thus there is a tradeoff to be recognized.

Charlotte opted for three-year terms, with a two consecutive term limit; Wichita Falls opted for two-year terms, while placing no limit on the number of consecutive terms. We view both choices as completely satisfactory. The comparative benefits of one over the other seem marginal.

Provisions for staff support for the board seem of critical importance. Too often this is neglected, and a board is dependent upon the handouts of the administration. As will be discussed further below, the board will receive technical and system-manager support from the data access control supervisor. However, the importance of competent clerical assistance can also be critical; this is best assured by requiring the office of the data access control supervisor to provide it. There is an added benefit in the fact that clerical assistants from that office will be continuously familiar with the subject matter and files.

DUTIES OF THE BOARD

VII. The Data Access Control Board shall be responsible for performing the duties listed below:

A. To implement the provisions of this ordinance.

B. To prepare and maintain sets of rules that in the aggregate constitute the elaboration of a formal Data Access Control System, all in consonance with the provisions of this ordinance, and for promulgation by the City Administration.

C. To function as an appellate body, holding hearings on administrative rulings by the Office of the City Manager with respect to data access control that are appealed to the Board by private citizens or private organizations.

D. To conduct inspections and audits of the Data Access Control System at such intervals and by such persons as may be required to assure its proper operation.

E. To recommend to the City Council such changes to this ordinance as in its judgment are warranted by future experience.

F. When necessary in its judgment, to conduct hearings with respect to the content of, or changes in the content of, Data Access Control Administrative Regulations and to conduct preliminary hearings with respect to contemplated recommended changes to this ordinance.

G. To cause to be prepared and published to the City Council a summary of all meetings and hearings conducted in executive session. Executive sessions may be used only for purposes of discussion. Meetings in which substantive decisions are made with respect to data access control shall be open to the public.

The data access control board is primarily a policy-setting unit. Policy is established within the limits of the authority expressed in the ordinance for implementation by the city administration. Implementation, in fact, will be the primary duty of the data access control supervisor, about which more will be said later in this chapter. However, responsibility to see that its policies are implemented remains with the board.

The most difficult task facing the board will be the preparation of the data access control administrative regulations. While these will be submitted in draft form by the data access control supervisor for review, revision, and approval by the board, the regulations will contain a sufficient number of decision points to require lengthy and thoughtful discussion by the board. More will be said about this in the following chapter.

While the board is responsible for the conduct of audits and inspections of the system, the board may or may not decide to participate in these activities. The board may feel that it is sufficient to provide for such activities and then verify that they are in fact being carried out in a satisfactory manner. On the other hand, should it decide to participate in audits and inspections, it is recommended that the board develop expert specializations to some extent among its members. Examples of useful specializations include physical security, fire protection, system auditing (including finance), and data storage protection.

Following the implementation of the system, the board will be faced with issues that cannot always be resolved within the city administration to the satisfaction of particular citizens or groups. These issues will be of four types: (1) requests for data that are denied; (2) objections to the release of data or to the level of protection they are given; (3) complaints about the accuracy or completeness of the data; and (4) requests for the deletion of data.

Requests for data are commonly made by university researchers, other governmental units, and various business and consulting firms. Very often such requests are for aggregations of personal data. Thus the board will have to decide whether or not the anonymity of individual records is adequately protected in each case and whether or not the data may be released.

Poorly designed systems or systems that are not rigorously supervised can result in the unauthorized distribution of personal data in the form of selected mailing lists by the members of the system. In some instances citizens have been able to trace their inclusion on mailing lists back to the city administration. Complaints of this nature are properly heard and resolved, either by the board or the data access control supervisor.

Complaints about the accuracy or completeness of the data are normally resolved by existing procedures within the city administration. However, where the complaint of the citizen is not satisfied by those procedures, the matter is appropriately brought to the board for determination.

Requests for the deletion of data will be less frequent, but they will occur. The most common example relates to records in the police department and the courts. This happens when the dispositions are not recorded of cases in which an individual is arrested but not brought to trial by the district attorney; in which an individual is brought to trial and the case results in a dismissal or acquittal; or in which an individual is convicted but the conviction is reversed on appeal. All of these instances involve failure to report final disposition to all those who maintain records relating to it. Frequently the problems are caused by "reporting lag" or by discontinuities in the reporting system. In any event, the board may, in meritorious cases, appropriately direct the deletion of data from records maintained by the city administration.

In all of these categories of cases, the board will require evidence from all parties to the issue. Sometimes this may be satisfied by a review of the statements submitted by the data access control supervisor and the complaining citizen, but more often it will require a hearing in which all parties receive adequate notice and are invited to attend for the purpose of presenting their positions. Anticipation of this supports the wisdom of devising, well in advance, the formal procedures that will govern the conduct of such hearings.

Monitoring the operation of the formal data access control system and conducting hearings for various purposes will result in the accumulation of much experience. Some of this experience will verify the adequacy and appropriateness of selected provisions of the data access control ordinance and administrative regulations; other experience will indicate the need for change in some of the provisions.

For example, the ordinance forbids the release of personal data; yet the production of selected mailing lists or the supplying to insurance companies of listings of persons receiving citations for moving violations, for example, can be a source of income to the city as well as a service for which there is demand. Should the board sense little opposition to certain of these practices, it may recommend that the pertinent provision of the ordinance be qualified so as to permit the exercise of the discretion of the board. Since this might appear to be delegating the legislative prerogative of the city council, the provision would have to be carefully framed, providing limits to the exercise of the board's discretion.

It is because of the controversial nature of questions concerning the release of personal data that the board needs to be empowered to hold hearings with respect to recommendations it may make to the city council for changes in the ordinance. Public hearings provide an opportunity to estimate the number of citizens who are really interested in the question and the intensity of their interest. The specialized competencies of the board members make it particularly appropriate to conduct such hearings and to react with appropriate recommendations to the city council, where, of course, hearings will again be held with respect to these recommendations.

It is doubtful that there will be much occasion for the board to hold hearings with respect to contemplated changes in administrative regulations. However, the authority is there should it be needed. The ordinance, having been expressed in general terms, leaves considerable latitude and discretion to the board with respect to implementation. It is conceivable that some of the policy questions of implementation will in themselves be controversial. Thus the board is equipped with the means for judging the extent of the potential for controversy by conducting hearings before making a decision about such policy questions.

One example is the question of charging for requested listings of public data. If no charge is made, a costly burden may be imposed on the city. If the charge is excessive, the policy may be regarded as discriminatory or even prohibitive, and thus in violation of the "open access to public records" provision of the ordinance. This provision may also be effectively violated by devising procedures for the request of public information that are excessively burdensome to the person making the request or, for that matter, that permit excessive amounts of time to pass before the requests are satisfied. The conduct of public hearings in the resolution of these questions can be very helpful in bypassing, or at least attentuating, controversy that otherwise might occur.

The final provision with respect to the duties of the board requires that the board prepare minutes of its meetings and that these be sent to the city council. Primarily because of the potential for controversy, it is important that the city council have the ability to monitor the activities of the board. The stipulation limiting the manner in which executive sessions may be used by the board is commonly accepted and should work no hardship on the board.

THE DATA ACCESS CONTROL SUPERVISOR

VIII. Creation of the Office of the Data Access Control Supervisor

    A. An Office of the Data Access Control Supervisor is hereby created to consist of the following personnel:
        1. Data Access Control Supervisor
        2. Systems Analyst-Programmer
        3. Clerk Typist
    B. The Data Access Control Supervisor shall report directly to the City Manager.

IX. Tasks of the Data Access Control Supervisor

The Data Access Control Supervisor shall be responsible for the tasks set forth below:

    A. To provide technical and clerical support for the Data Access Control Board.

    B. To prepare drafts of Data Access Control Administrative Regulations and timely changes thereto and drafts of changes to this ordinance as the need occurs, such drafts being prepared for consideration by the Board.

    C. To exercise ongoing general supervision and management of the Data Access Control System, ensuring continuing compliance with the provisions of this ordinance and with the Data Access Control Administrative Regulations.
    D. To conduct detailed periodic and random inspections of the system and its parts, correcting deficiencies and reporting instances of noncompliance to the City Manager.

E. To maintain and cause to be maintained, as appropriate, a system of records that ensures an audit trail of the activities of the Office of the Data Access Control Supervisor and of the data that is entered, stored, processed, or released by the Data Access Control System.

F. To maintain liaison with the Fire Department and Police Department so as to ensure expert participation in fire and physical security inspections of the system and in the evaluations and recommendations deriving therefrom.

G. To advise the City Manager and the Board of the condition of the system and of changes in the reported condition.

H. To maintain liaison with the City Attorney so as to be continuously informed of the laws with which the system must be in compliance.

I. To perform such other tasks as may appropriately be assigned by the City Manager.

The personnel assignments to the office of the data access control supervisor will probably raise a question only with respect to the programmer-analyst. These skills are required for a number of purposes: (1) to assist the supervisor in developing the formal system; (2) to assist in the audit of software; (3) to review programs for audit-trail adequacy; (4) to develop standard program specifications with respect to audit trails, reasonableness checks, security checks, validation checks, and so on; and (5) to provide technical advice to the supervisor in matters relating to software and system flows.

The most difficult task of the supervisor will be to prepare the initial draft of administrative regulations. In so doing, he should highlight significant policy questions for the board's attention and be prepared to discuss the range of alternatives and the relative merits of each candidate solution to a policy question.

In coordination with the city manager, the supervisor will be able to influence the pace of development of the regulations and also the approach to be used. For example, it is preferable that the broad shape of the system be developed first, and thereafter the interstitial development of the details.

In addition to the preparation of administrative regulations, the supervisor is responsible for the ongoing operation of the system, for the maintenance of required records, for the scheduling and conduct of inspections, and for the reporting of instances of noncompliance to the city manager.

Through liaison with the city attorney and through his own research, the supervisor is responsible for keeping himself informed of all laws, statutes, and ordinances that impinge upon data access control, including those that are currently under consideration by relevant legislative bodies. The supervisor must ensure that the developed system is in continuing compliance with the law.

The supervisor has line authority with respect to his own office, but he exercises control of personnel participating in the data access control system through the city manager.

FURTHER EXAMPLES

The reader is referred to Appendixes A and B for further examples of data access control ordinances, namely those of Wichita Falls and Charlotte.

9

DATA ACCESS CONTROL
ADMINISTRATIVE REGULATIONS

DIVERSITY AND AN UNSETTLED TAXONOMY

Data access control regulations are contained in a lengthy, detailed document that structures the formal data access control system within the governing provisions of the data access control ordinance. It not only structures the system, providing for the numerous procedures and rules that are required, but it also provides for a variety of audits and inspections of the system.

However, when we delineate procedures for each element and subelement of the system, we are getting down to a level of detail that permits little similarity in the administrative regulations of cities across the country. This is understandable, given the varieties of data processing environments that exist in the different cities.

To illustrate, a number of cities rely on bureau services, while others contain their operations in-house; some develop their own software, while others rely on vendor supplied software and thus may have no programming capability of their own; many cities have very small shops that perform a few finance, personnel, or utility billing applications, while others have very large installations performing tasks for virtually every department of the city administration; some cities have centralized their data processing into one location, while others have widely separated computer systems; some decentralized systems are centralized with respect to management, while others are not; some systems are on-line real-time, while others may be on-line scheduled, or perhaps not on-line at all; some are computer batch operations, while others may also be remote batch; some are large enough to require a high degree of job specialization and many formal relationships, while others are so small that each employee performs in a number of roles.

Although we might extend this list of illustrations even further by considering the varieties of municipalities and other matters, this listing should be sufficient to illustrate that since administrative regulations must be tailored to the data processing environment of a given city, and since these environments are so different, it necessarily follows that a model of administrative regulations would totally mislead the reader. What should be helpful would be a general discussion of the desired content of administrative regulations and an example.

We have selected the Charlotte example as the one that is the most complete and detailed. It is appended to this handbook, not as a model for emulation but as a useful example. (See Appendix D.)

But a word of caution: This subject area is still so new that the taxonomy is unsettled. The documents "Data Access Control Plan," "Data Access Control Resolution," "Data Access Control Ordinance," and "Data Access Control Administrative Regulations" all have different content when those of Wichita Falls are compared with those of Charlotte and with the discussions contained in this text. For example, Charlotte's "Data Access Control Plan" is to us a consolidation of an ordinance and of administrative regulations, but not a plan as we have defined it.

This unsettled taxonomy also extends to those who perform prominent roles in data access control. For example, what we have chosen to call a "data access control board" is the "data access advisory board" in Wichita Falls and the "municipal information review board" in Charlotte. And what we call a "data access control supervisor" is the "data registrar" in Wichita Falls and the "municipal information officer" in Charlotte.

However, this state of affairs should work no real hardship on the reader. We do see merit in some degree of standardization of terms, and for that reason we recommend those contained in this handbook for consideration. On the other hand, the diversity of terminology that now exists does suggest a measure of flexibility and choice available to a system designer to help him cope with local preferences.

For all of the reasons discussed above, we will depart in this chapter from the format of earlier chapters, in which we presented models of specific documents. Therefore, in this chapter we will discuss only the general content of administrative regulations.

GENERAL CONTENT

Administrative regulations will generally constitute an expansion of the provisions of the data access control ordinance, together with the delineation of procedures by which the ordinance can be implemented. This suggests the following list of broad headings:

- Purpose of a Data Access Control System
- General Standards
- Levels of Data Classification
- Description of Operating Environment
- Procedures, Rules and Forms
- Audit Trail Requirements
- Monitoring and Inspections
- Standards of Ethics
- Penalties for Noncompliance

Purpose

The purpose of a data access control system is to establish procedures, subject to such limitations as may exist in law, whereby the public will be assured of access to public data and also be assured of privacy with respect to the personal data the city collects about its citizens. The language for this section may be taken verbatim from the data access control ordinance; as a minimum the ordinance should be referenced in, or appended to, the administrative regulations.

General Standards

General standards, as described in the ordinance, constitute broadly expressed rules that, if followed, are implementive of the purpose as expressed in the preceeding section. The procedures defined in administrative regulations will necessarily address these standards in the most direct way possible. It is advisable to extract the general standards from the ordinances and have them set forth in this section, even though the ordinance may be appended to administrative regulations.

Levels of Classification

The levels of classification of data, with corresponding levels of protection, should be defined in this section of the administrative regulations. The data access control supervisor and the date access control board may anticipate some difficulty in producing those definitions.

At first glance it would seem that an arbitrary range of classifications could be assigned, each level in the range providing for higher degrees of protection than the one below it. After considerable study of the problem this is in fact what Charlotte chose to do. Charlotte provided for three access categories: public, restricted, and highly restricted. The rules with respect to each are summarized below:

Public. This information is open for inspection by any person at any reasonable time.

Restricted. This information is open to city employees who require it in the performance of their official duties; other persons granted access by the data access control board; and, if it is personal information, to the individual to whom it refers.

Highly Restricted. This information is open only to persons involved in the performance of the public function for which the information was originally collected or produced. In other words, this is the same as Restricted, except that access to two categories of persons has been deleted.

Wichita Falls, on the other hand, chose an entirely different approach, defining the data that could or could not be released on a department by department basis, after first setting forth the general rules that would apply.

It is actually desirable to combine both approaches. The Charlotte levels of classification are not, for example, incompatible with the Wichita Falls department by department approach, but rather constitute a convenient generalization of the rules into three categories of access eligibility. The elaboration of those rules would have to be done in any case. Each data element or family of data elements, such as one might find on a single form collected or produced by each department, must be explicated. Also there is considerable merit in establishing general rules for access to data collected or produced by each department (or function), since this serves to give emphasis and to put one on guard.

Examples of both approaches are contained in Appendix D of the Wichita Falls Material (see Appendix A) and Section 6 of the Charlotte material (see Appendix B).

Description of Operating Environment

There are four perspectives to any operating environment of a data access control system: organization, manual data processing, automated data processing; and personnel. Each of these should be described to the extent that it influences the shape and nature of the procedures to be followed in the data access control system.

Organization: The organizational perspective should address the hierarchy of the city government, including the role and tasks of the data access control board and the data access control supervisor and their relationship to the rest of the city organization.

This will vary according to such factors as whether or not the municipal form of government is councilmanic, with an appointed or elected executive; whether or not members of the data access control board are appointed from the city administration, the council, the general public, or a mix of the three; what status is given the data access control supervisor, such as a line or a staff relationship to the city manager; and what is the organizational and hierarchical relationship of the data processing shop(s) to the city manager. There are many other considerations that ought to be made explicit before developing the procedures that will apply in the operation of the system.

Manual Data Processing: The manual data processing perspective of the data access control environment continues to be important, more so in fact where automated data processing is employed. This is because one of the end products of the computer is hard copy output. In most instances this has resulted in a demand for much more manual file space than was required in a fully manual system of operation. Thus it needs to be recognized that the data access control system will address both manual and automated processing perspectives.

With respect to manual data processing, however, this means that the availability and description of the various kinds of facilities for manual storage needs to be set forth. This includes the definition of levels of security with respect to certain kinds of storage facilities, from unlockable filing cabinets to fireproof, high security safes. It also includes the association of these depositories with particular offices in the organizational structure.

Automated Data Processing: The automated data processing perspective should address hardware, software, communications, and peripherals (such as teletypes, CRTs, and remote printers) utilized by the city for data processing. These may be distributed widely or consolidated into one shop, and they may be decentralized with respect to operations and management but centralized with respect to the rules and procedures of data access control.

The location, organizational and physical, of data processing should be described, together with the levels of physical security available to it. Concerning these latter it should include a description of both fire and burglar alarms, local and remote fire protection equipment, local and remote police protection, and internal security devices other than these.

Personnel: Finally, the personnel perspective of the data access control system should address the classes of personnel in the city administration in terms of data handling and measures taken to ensure the proper handling of that data. Specifically, this requires the identification of those groups of personnel in the organization that are required to signify that they have read, understood, and agreed to abide by the statement of ethics with respect to data handling.

This perspective also requires the identification by groups or classes of those personnel who are required to submit to background investigations or who must be bonded before being assigned information handling duties.

It is the description of the total data access control environment that influences the level of additional security that must be defined in procedures, the additional provisions required for coordination, the required intensity and frequency of monitoring and inspecting, and the level of detail and distribution of reports. The validity of the procedures will be tested continuously against, and understood with respect to, the environmental description.

Procedures, Rules, and Forms

The data access control system consists essentially of the aggregate of all of the procedures defined for the operation of the system. Each procedure embodies the rules and identifies the persons to whom the rules relate for the execution of the procedure. Where the procedure is exercised on a routine basis, basic forms need to be designed and used in order to assure uniformity and regularity.

The most immediate concern in developing the system will be to identify and control the data base. This must be done systematically by designing a form that identifies the kind of data, its source, where and how it is filed, the purpose for which it is collected, the security classification if any, and the persons authorized to receive the data. This form should be completed for all the data the city collects. The same form can be used on a continuing basis when a department applies either for authorization to collect additional kinds of data or for data from another department, as the need may arise.

Somewhat different procedures and forms need to be devised for the accommodation of ad hoc requests for data. These will differ according to whether the request is made by a member of the administration or the general public. Fee schedules will be needed in order to establish the amount to be charged, if any, to members of the general public for data that they request.

Procedures and forms will be needed to accomplish security classification changes, whether for purposes of upgrading or downgrading existing classifications of data. Similarly, procedures and forms will be required in order to create a security classification for new kinds of data that are to be collected on a continuing basis beginning at some specified time in the future. Requests for data classification may be initiated by the data access control supervisor, by a department in the administration, or by a member of the general public.

There will be a requirement for procedures and forms to initiate and process appeals to the data access control board by members of the general public. Such an appeal may be with reference to either an ad hoc or a continuing request for access to data that has been refused by the data access control supervisor.

Conversely, such an appeal may result from an unsuccessful request by a member of the general public to have the classification of particular data upgraded or for additional measures of security to be provided to protect personal data. Then, too, the procedures themselves may be appealed as excessively burdensome, slow, or expensive.

Receipting procedures and forms will be needed. These may vary according to the media in which the file is represented or stored, such as hard copy or punch cards, tape or disk pack. They may also vary according to whether or not the procedures provide for follow-up checks so as to ensure a capability for establishing the location of all files of data at any one time.

Procedures will be required for validating remote terminals and operators where these are used in the system and for validating the authorization of an operator to have access to particular files or programs. It should be remembered that even where an operator is found to be authorized to call for a particular file, it must yet be established whether that authorization is to "read only" or "read and write." A read and write authorization permits the operator to input data to the file, to make deletions, or to make other changes in the data of the file being worked. These validation procedures can be fully automated in the system.

There also will be a requirement for standardized marking procedures on classified files of data, and these markings will differ according to the medium in which the data is stored. Marking of hard copy files, for example, can be rubber-stamped, but tape reels and disk packs will need to be tagged or marked in some other fashion. The procedures should provide for the means of disposal of classified data contained on hard copy and, when appropriate, for the purging of data stored in tapes or disks.

Finally, procedures will need to be planned for coping with various emergencies that might arise. These include bomb threats, riot, earthquake, fire, power loss, and air-conditioning failure. The procedures should be published, and the personnel involved in using them should be required to participate in training sessions at regular intervals to ensure that they understand the importance of complying with the regulations and procedures.

Audit Trail Requirements

In order to permit a reconstruction of the activities that occur in the data access control system, it will be necessary to devise a schedule of records and reports appropriate for each part of the system. At the level of the data access control board this requirement would be satisfied by a compilation of the board's minutes, together with a journal of its activities that includes the dates, times, and purposes of the meetings, hearings, inspections, or other official activities it performs as a body.

At the level of the data access control supervisor this requirement would be met by files of the completed forms on which data access or data classification has been requested and action taken and by files of the forms used for the conduct of inspections of the system or its parts. These should record the results, together with the follow-up actions taken. A journal should be maintained that identifies applications received, actions taken, and the dates of each; it should also contain the continuing history of inspections, including dates and places. A register cataloging all of the data collected by the city should be established and maintained.

Audit trail requirements are substantial within the data processing unit, but satisfaction of most of the requirements can be automated. Here, the requirement is for at least the following four types of audit trails: (1) an ability to reconstruct the receipt and delivery of data files to and from data processing over a period of time and the processing the files have received internally; (2) an ability to reconstruct the files themselves as they existed in some past point in time, as may be required; (3) a record of programs and program modifications; and (4) a record of all remote entries or attempted entries into the system and the programs and files accessed.

Most of the foregoing may be satisfied by the maintenance of a system of receipts and a log of activity. Where log maintenance is automated, the file (tape, disk, or core storage) should be dumped (represented on hard copy) periodically for review in data processing and for review by the data access control supervisor. However, any attempt to make unauthorized access to the system should be brought to the attention of the data access control supervisor immediately, even though it would again be reported at some later point in a review of the log.

Procedures should be published to the departments of the city administration, providing for the receipting and logging of selected categories of data received and released. This will normally be required only with respect to files of data, but in some instances it will be required for individual records. A typical example would be a requirement for a receipt and a log-out for each file of hard copy records en route to data processing.

Monitoring and Inspecting

The burden of monitoring and inspecting the operation of the data access control system will of course fall upon the data access control supervisor. The regulations should identify the documents he is to review and the processes he is to observe on a continuing basis in order to satisfy the monitoring function.

The regulations should also identify the kinds and the periodicity of inspections he is expected to make or have made. These include routine and ad hoc inspections for fire hazards, checks on physical security, emergency drills, audits of the system, and verifications of procedures. Each kind of inspection should be made on the basis of appropriately designed but open-ended check-off lists. Inspection planning should include identification of the members of the inspection party for each type. For example, a particular inspection party might include the data access control board, the finance auditor, and the fire and/or police representative as well as the data access control supervisor.

Standards of Ethics

The data access control administrative regulations should contain a section on the ethical standards to be met by information handlers. It should be general enough to be equally applicable to data processing personnel and the personnel who handle only hard copy data. Provisions should be made for the certification by each employee that he has read and understands the statement of ethics.

Following is a model statement of ethics that may be used as a point of departure in formulating standards for local use.

STATEMENT OF ETHICS

As an employee of the City of_____, I understand the importance of protecting the confidentiality of personal or otherwise classified data collected by the city that may from time to time come into my possession. To this end, I am bound by the provisions of the Data Access Control Ordinance and the Data Access Control Administrative Regulations, both of which have been made available for my review.
In particular, I agree to the following:
1. I will take all reasonable precautions to ensure the security of the classified files, records, and information that are in my possession.

2. I will not use classified information for purposes other than required by my official duties.

3. I will not permit other persons to have access to classified files or classified information that is in my possession, except as may be required in the perfor-mance of their official duties.

4. I will take all reasonable precautions to ensure that data that I enter or cause to be entered into a file is accurate and complete and required to be so entered in the performance of my official duties.

5. It is my duty to report infractions of the foregoing by others when knowledge of such infractions comes to my attention.

I hereby acknowledge that I have read and certify all of the foregoing.

Date	Employee's Signature

Penalties for Noncompliance

The concluding section of administrative regulations should contain provisions for penalties. These may relate to misconduct in office resulting in personnel action for suspension, dismissal, or other penalties as may be provided for in existing civil service regulations. The penalties section may additionally provide that violation of the ordinance shall constitute a misdemeanor for which a fine and imprisonment may be imposed. The penalties section should be rigorously consistent with the provisions of the ordinance, civil service regulations, and such other regulations as may apply. (See the section on penalties in Chapter 8 for further discussion.)

FURTHER EXAMPLES

For an example of data access control administrative regulations, see Appendix D (Charlotte), but note that the regulations are identified as a "Data Access Control Plan." For an example of data access control board internal procedures, see Appendix E (Wichita Falls).

CITY OF WICHITA FALLS

Ordinance No. 2688
An Ordinance Creating a Data Access Control Plan

WHEREAS, the City of Wichita Falls is building a municipal information system, which includes the computerization of urban records, which will greatly simplify access to such records; and,

WHEREAS, it is the intention of the City Council that the data which will be entered into such municipal information system will be only the operationally oriented data of the City of Wichita Falls and various other local government organizations, and no data will be put into the system which is not used operationally or analytically by the City and other local governments; and,

WHEREAS, it is the desire of the City Council to protect the privacy of individuals by limiting access to such computerized records, while at the same time complying with Section 131 of the Charter of the City of Wichita Falls which provides that all accounts and records of every office and department of the City shall be open to the public at all reasonable times, except the records and documents from which might be secured information which might defeat the lawful purpose of the officer or department withholding them from access of the public.

NOW, THEREFORE, BE IT ORDAINED BY THE BOARD OF ALDERMEN OF THE CITY OF WICHITA FALLS, TEXAS, THAT:

SECTION 1. The following data access control plan is hereby adopted by the City of Wichita Falls, and shall be complied with by the officers and employees of the City of Wichita Falls. This ordinance applies only to records controlled and maintained on the computer system, and applies to all requests for information, by City officers and employees as well as the general public.

SECTION 2. The City Manager shall appoint an employee of substantial responsibility, who reports directly to the City Manager, to the position of Data Registrar. Requests for the release of information, except for normal routine requests by City operational departments for information necessary to carry out their functions, and except for routine requests for information which has been traditionally available to the general public, will be directed to the Data Registrar, who shall either approve or disapprove such requests

85

in accordance with the guidelines established in this ordinance. All such requests will be in writing on a form provided by the Data Registrar, which form will state the date, name and address of the party requesting the information, the ultimate use to be made of the information, and any other pertinent facts. In the event the Data Registrar is unavailable, an acting Data Registrar shall be appointed by the City Manager to serve in his place.

Each request for information shall be delivered to the Data Registrar during normal business hours, and shall be either approved or disapproved by him within 24 hours, unless the end of the 24 hours falls on a Saturday, Sunday or legal holiday, in which event such approval or disapproval shall be given at such hour on the next day which is not such Saturday, Sunday or legal holiday.

If such request is approved, the requested information will be delivered as soon as it can be prepared without interfering with the normal operations of the affected departments of the City.

If such request is disapproved by the Data Registrar, he shall notify the person requesting the information of such action, together with his reason for such disapproval.

Whenever such information is delivered to the person requesting it, such person shall pay to the City a fee for such information. A schedule of fees shall be established by the City Manager, which schedule will be available to the public. The purpose of the fee shall be to reimburse the City for the cost of the effort required to produce information not normally available through routine operations.

The Data Registrar shall maintain a record of each request for the release of information, which record will contain the name of the party requesting the information, the date of the request, the purpose for which the information is requested, the final disposition of the request, and any other information deemed necessary.

SECTION 3. There is hereby created a Data Access Advisory Board, hereafter referred to as the Board. It shall be composed of five (5) members, who shall serve without pay. The members shall be appointed by the Mayor, and the appointments must be approved by the Board of Aldermen. The terms of such members shall be for two (2) years, beginning on the first day of January; however, the initial terms shall be staggered so that two members' terms shall expire December 31, 1972 and three members' terms shall expire December 31, 1973. Each member shall serve until his successor has been appointed and approved. The Mayor, with the approval of the Board of Aldermen, shall appoint one of the members as Chairman.

SECTION 3.1. The Board shall have the following duties:

A. To advise the Data Registrar and the Board of Aldermen regarding controls and policies affecting the release of information.

B. To assist the Data Registrar and the Board of Aldermen in establishing criteria to determine the "need to know" test.

C. To assist the Data Registrar in establishing ethics regarding requests for specific types of information.

D. To consider any expansion of the data base which will result in acquisition and storage of data not previously maintained by the City, and to advise the Board of Aldermen with reference thereto.

SECTION 4. Any person on whom data is accumulated and filed shall have the right to review such data for accuracy upon making such a request to the Data Registrar, and paying the prescribed fee, if applicable. This shall guarantee to such person the right to correct any inaccurate data. If the accuracy of any data is questioned, the City will confirm the accuracy of the source document, as well as the conversion to computerized records. Any questioned data shall be frozen with respect to dissemination for a reasonable time until the accuracy or inaccuracy of that data is established. Upon receipt of proof that any such data is inaccurate, it shall be corrected.

SECTION 5. When the purpose of any request for information is to obtain evidence to be used in the trial of a lawsuit, such request shall be directed by the Data Registrar to the City Attorney who shall advise the Registrar as to whether or not such request should be approved. In the event such request is disapproved, it shall be necessary for the person requesting such information to obtain same through the use of a subpoena.

SECTION 6. Any requested information which is not identifiable to any individual, is not restricted by Sections 8 through 8.5, and which will not defeat the lawful purpose of the City officer or department responsible for the information, may be released.

SECTION 7. Information which is identifiable to any particular person will not be released to anyone, other than that person or any other person who has a legitimate need to know such information. The criteria of the "need to know" test shall be administered by the Data Registrar.

SECTION 8. The data which is collected by the Department of Vital Statistics, Department of Personnel, Police Department, Fire Prevention Bureau and Public Health Department shall not be released except as specified in Sections 8.1 through 8.5.

SECTION 8.1. Department of Vital Statistics: No information concerning illegitimacy or adoption certificates shall be released except upon the order of a court of competent jurisdiction. Information concerning birth and death certificates and name changes shall be released only to properly qualified applicants, who shall include only law enforcement personnel, insurance agencies (death certificates only), attorneys at law (when representing a client who is the subject of the data), and close relatives of the person whose records are being requested.

SECTION 8.2. Personnel Department: Generally, the files of this department are regarded as confidential. Information from such files shall be released only to law enforcement agencies and agencies responsible for national security and others who, in the opinion of the Data Registrar, have a legitimate need to know such information. In addition, information from the file of an employee shall be released to his department head or prospective department head or any other officer or employee of the City, who, in the opinion of the Data Registrar, has a legitimate need to know such information.

SECTION 8.3. Police Department: The sensitive data maintained by the Police Department has been grouped into eight categories; three of these are fully confidential. The data which is fully confidential shall be released to no one (including the person who is the subject of the data) outside the chain of prosecution and law enforcement agencies. The data which is semi-confidential shall be released to no one other than the person who is the subject of the data, law enforcement agencies, the prosecuting attorneys and the defense attorneys. The three categories of data which are fully confidential are the officers' reports, the juvenile reports and the supplementary officers' reports; the five categories of data which are semi-confidential are the criminal arrest records, the complaint reports, the traffic accident reports, complaints concerning police officers, and information concerning bomb reports.

SECTION 8.4. Fire Prevention Bureau: Data concerning arson investigation reports shall not be released to anyone other than personnel engaged in arson investigation and prosecution and to law enforcement agencies.

SECTION 8.5. Public Health Department: Information concerning the medical records of individuals shall not be released to anyone other than the individual, except on the written approval of the Director of the Department.

SECTION 8.6. Whenever any information described in Sections 8.1 through 8.5 has been released, the Director under whose responsibility the data is gathered and maintained shall be notified of such release, and to whom the information is released.

SECTION 9. Information which will defeat the lawful purpose of the City officer or department responsible for such information shall not be released.

SECTION 10. Any person who is dissatisfied with the administration of the policies covered by this ordinance may appeal such actions to the Board of Aldermen at a regularly scheduled meeting.

SECTION 11. Any employee of the City of Wichita Falls who violates any of the provisions of this ordinance shall be subject to administrative disciplinary action, up to and including termination.

SECTION 12. Notwithstanding the provisions of any other section herein restricting the release of information, the Data Registrar and other employees of the City having custody or control of data covered by this ordinance shall produce and release any information if and as directed by the lawful order of a court of competent jurisdiction.

SECTION 13. The provisions of this ordinance shall be included and incorporated in the Code of Ordinances of the City of Wichita Falls as an addition thereto, and shall be appropriately renumbered to conform to the uniform numbering system of the Code.

PASSED AND APPROVED THIS THE 15 day of February, 1972.

CITY OF CHARLOTTE
ORDINANCE CREATING A MUNICIPAL
INFORMATION REVIEW BOARD AND ESTABLISHING
A MUNICIPAL INFORMATION POLICY

Section 1. Municipal Information Review Board—Created; membership; vacancies

There is established a Municipal Information Review Board
whose duty it is to supervise the collection, storage, usage and dissemination of information collected, produced, stored, used or disseminated by the City of Charlotte. The Board has seven members
appointed by the Mayor to three-year terms. The Mayor shall designate
one of the appointees to be chairman. Terms begin on _____.
Members shall serve without compensation. No member may serve
more than two consecutive three-year terms. The Mayor shall fill
any vacancy for the unexpired term.

A majority of the membership of the Board constitutes a
quorum.

Section 2. Powers and duties

The Municipal Information Review Board shall:
a. Supervise collection, production, storage, usage and
    dissemination of information collected, stored, used or
    disseminated by the City of Charlotte.
b. Approve safeguard techniques for the maintenance of
    information developed by the Municipal Information
    Department and may issue such rules and regulations
    as are necessary to implement these techniques.
c. Adopt procedures for appeals to the Board.
d. Review annually the nature of the information that is
    being collected, stored, used or disseminated by the
    city and the classification of the information.
e. Establish regulations governing the collection, storage,
    use and dissemination of information and recommend
    to the Council which of those ought to be enacted as
    ordinances of the city.

Section 3. Staff

The Director of the Municipal Information Department of the
city is the staff assistant to the Board and shall perform the tasks
required of him by the Board.

Section 4. Municipal Information System—Definitions
   a. "Municipal information" means any information col-
       lected, stored, used or disseminated by any depart-
       ment, agency, board or commission of the City of
       Charlotte, or any information stored in or trans-
       mitted through the city's computerized municipal
       information system.
   b. "Personal information" means information about
       specific persons where the persons about whom the
       information is maintained are identifiable.
   c. "Non-Personal information" means information not
       about specific persons or information about persons
       where those persons are not identifiable.
Section 5. Collection of Personal Information
       No department, agency, board or commission of the City of
Charlotte may collect personal information unless it has obtained
approval for collection from the Municipal Information Review Board.
The Board may grant approval for the collection only if the department, agency, board or commission has shown that it has a proper
governmental purpose for collecting the information and the information to be collected is rationally related to that proper purpose.
Section 6. Classification; access
   a. All municipal information shall be placed in one of
       the following three access categories: (1) public,
       (2) restricted, or (3) highly restricted.
   b. Information placed in the public access category shall
       be open for inspection by any person at reasonable
       times and copies shall be furnished upon payment of
       reasonable fees as fixed by the City Council.
   c. Information placed in the restricted access category
       shall be open to the following classes of persons at
       reasonable times: (1) persons in the department,
       agency, board or commission involved in the per-
       formance of the public function for which the infor-
       mation was originally collected or produced, (2)
       other persons who have been granted access by the
       Municipal Information Review Board because they
       have shown a proper governmental purpose for use
       of the information, and (3) if the information is
       personal information, the individual about whom
       the information is maintained.
   d. Information placed in the highly restricted category
       shall be open only to those persons involved in the
       performance of the public function for which the
       information was originally collected or produced.

Section 7. Category Placement

The Municipal Information Review Board shall determine the category placement of information. The Board shall place personal information in the restricted access category except as follows: (a) if there is a specific statute requiring the information to be maintained as public record, the Board shall place the information in the public access category, or (b) if the department, agency, board or commission collecting the information presents to the Board a compelling public purpose for denying access to the individual about whom the information is maintained, the Board shall place the information in the highly restricted category.

The Board shall place non-personal information in the public access category except that it may place the information in the restricted category in the following cases: (a) if a specific statute requires the information to be restricted to certain persons or (b) if the department, agency, board or commission collecting or producing the information presents to the Board a compelling public purpose for limiting access to the information.

Section 8. Access to restricted information by persons other than the collecting agency

   a. A department, agency, board or commission of the City of Charlotte, other than the one originally collecting or producing the information, or a department, agency, board or commission of another governmental unit may have access to information placed in the restricted category only if access is approved by the Municipal Information Review Board. The Board may approve access if the department, agency, board or commission seeking access has shown a proper governmental purpose for use of the information.

   b. A person not acting in the performance of duties as a municipal employee, other than an individual seeking access to information about himself, that wants access to restricted information is required to have such access approved by the Board. The Board may approve access if the person seeking access has shown a proper public purpose for the use of the information.

   c. A person has the right of access to information pertaining directly to him that is maintained in the restricted access category. A person is entitled to add to or correct the information pertaining to him upon the presentation of identification and proof of the correction to the department, agency, board or commission of the City of Charlotte that collected or produced the information.

Section 9. Request for access

The head of the department, agency, board or commission that collects or produces information is the custodian of that information. A request for access to public records by any person or for access to restricted information by an approved person shall be made to the custodian or his designee. The custodian or his designee shall grant access to any person entitled to access under this ordinance.

Section 10. Appeals

Appeals from action by officers and employees of the City of Charlotte in the performance of their duties of collecting, storing, using or disseminating municipal information shall be to the Municipal Information Review Board.

Section 11. Register

The Municipal Information Department shall maintain a register of all information collected, produced or stored by the City of Charlotte. The register shall set forth, with respect to each department, agency, board or commission collecting, producing or storing information: (1) the name and location of the department, agency, board or commission; (2) the head of the department, agency, board or commission, and if there is one, the person designated as record keeper; (3) the nature of information collected, produced or stored; (4) the access categories into which each type of information is placed; and (5) the classes of persons for whom access is authorized.

The register shall be open for inspection by any person at reasonable times.

Section 12. Misuse of personal information

A person authorized to collect or have access to personal information shall not:

(a) Give this information to persons for whom access has not been authorized;

(b) Use this information for any purpose other than that purpose for which the Municipal Information Review Board authorized collection or access.

Section 13. Violations

No person may willfully collect, produce, store, use, disseminate or gain access to municipal information except in accordance with this ordinance.

A person about whom information is being collected, stored, used or disseminated in violation of this ordinance may enjoin the collection, storage, usage or dissemination by an action for injunction.

Section 14. Applicability

Sections 5 through 13 of this ordinance apply to each department, agency, board and commission of the City of Charlotte when the Municipal Information Review Board reviews the information collected, produced, stored, used or disseminated by the department, agency, board or commission and determines the category placement of that information.

February 8, 1965

CITY OF DAYTON
DIVISION OF TAXATION

To:

Subject: Confidential Nature of Income Tax Information

Your attention is directed to Section 9D of Ordinance 21420 (commonly referred to as the Dayton Income Tax Ordinance) which recites that all information received by the Division of Taxation is confidential and is to be disclosed to no one except in the normal course of business. In order that you may be fully aware of the provisions of the Ordinance regarding this matter, Section 9D is reproduced in full below.

> Any information gained as the result of any returns, investigations, hearings, or verifications required or authorized by this Ordinance shall be confidential, except for official purposes, or except when ordered by a Court of competent jurisdiction. Any person divulging such information in violation of this Ordinance, shall, upon conviction thereof, be deemed guilty of a misdemeanor and shall be subject to a fine or penalty of not more than Five Hundred Dollars ($500.00) or imprisoned for not more than six (6) months, or both. Each disclosure shall constitute a separate offense.
>
> In addition to the above penalty, any employee of the City of Dayton who violates the provisions of this Section relative to the disclosure of confidential information shall be guilty of an offense punishable by immediate dismissal.

To make certain that there may be no misunderstanding on your part regarding this matter, you are hereby advised that the above Section of the Ordinance provides that no disclosure of information shown on tax returns, including withholding statements, be made to persons outside the Division of Taxation or these with whom it is necessary to show the information in order to implement

95

the work of the Division, and also no disclosure of information shall be made in the normal course of Division's work unless such disclosure is required in conjunction with the work of the Division. Any employee of the Division of Taxation or any other employee of the City found guilty of disclosing information relative to returns with other employees of the Division or in the City, where such disclosure is not required in the performance of regularly assigned duties, will be subject to immediate dismissal.

Although Ordinance 21420 did not become effective until January 1, 1965, all prior Dayton Income Tax Ordinances carry the same provisions and information relative to tax returns for years prior to 1965 shall also be treated confidentially.

To make certain that you have read and understand the contents of this memorandum, it is being issued in duplicate and you are requested to sign one copy and return it to me promptly. If you have any questions regarding this memorandum, please feel free to discuss them with me.

/s/ _____

Superintendent, Division of
Taxation

I hereby acknowledge that I have read the foregoing and I am aware of the provisions of the Dayton Income Tax Ordinances regarding the confidential nature of information received by the Division of Taxation and of the consequences of disclosing such information.

_____

Employee's Signature

_____

Date

THE CHARLOTTE MIS DEPARTMENT
DATA ACCESS CONTROL PLAN
USAC CNCO 0127
MIS-8203/000/01
January 1973

Prepared by
The City of Charlotte, North Carolina
The University of North Carolina
System Development Corporation

For the
DEPARTMENT OF HOUSING AND URBAN DEVELOPMENT
Contract No. H-1216
CHARLOTTE INTEGRATED MUNICIPAL INFORMATION
SYSTEM PROJECT

INTRODUCTION

This document establishes a methodology for the control of data access within the municipal government environment of Charlotte, North Carolina.

In developing the content of this Data Access Control Plan (DACP), supporting studies were conducted to examine significant legal, social, and policy considerations associated with municipal data. Particular attention was given to the questions of privacy, confidentiality and security in relation to the computer storage and manipulation of data within Charlotte's Integrated Municipal Information System (IMIS).

In addition to their being incorporated in the Data Access Control Plan, results of a number of studies have been published as separate reports.*

---

*The reports listed below were prepared for the Charlotte IMIS Project by consortium members at the University of North Carolina, Chapel Hill:

Barr, Joel, Public Records: Privacy and Access. July 19, 1971.

The work in this general task area made it apparent that the data access control problem has many facets, which are reflected in the Plan itself. A few of the more important considerations which have influenced the organization and emphasis of this Plan are discussed below.

General Considerations

Major objectives which the City of Charlotte has accepted for its municipal data access control program are: (a) protecting the privacy of information which should be kept confidential and (b) providing ready departmental and public access to public records.

In examining ways to meet the major objectives for the IMIS, it was evident at the outset that any effective control of IMIS data must involve, at a minimum, those user departments and others who might collect or handle the same data. Additionally, a program which considers only automated data is likely to fall far short of meeting the real objectives, since the basic problem exists equally for data which are maintained in manual forms. This problem will continue to exist during the foreseeable future. From the citizens' point of view, the differences between automated and manual information should be unrelated to the end results of an access control program. The real problem, one which has been highlighted by the advent of increasing automation, has as its natural focus all municipal information.

The City of Charlotte has adopted the premise that the Data Access Control Plan for the IMIS must be an integral part of a larger program for the city as a whole. The DACP cannot realistically be confined to the Municipal Information System Department and its automated system. This broader orientation clearly expands the scope of the DACP, and clearly introduces additional questions of economic, political, and technical feasibility. However, because it is essential to the success of any program for the IMIS, major initial phases of the task have been devoted to developing a Plan at a level

---

Barr, Joel, and Hemmens, George C. Analysis of Existing Departmental Policies and Practices Regarding Public Records and Confidentiality. October 1, 1971.

Tucker, Robert B., Jr. Legal Considerations on the Collection, Use and Dissemination of Computerized Personal Data: An overview.

Stallings, C. Wayne. A Confidentiality and Public Access Policy for Local Government. August 1972.

of city-wide involvement. The Plan presented in this document reflects that emphasis.

As outlined below, sections of the basic Plan are concerned with establishing a framework of principles and procedures which apply to the City as a whole. That general framework, when adopted, provides a known municipal environment in which to continue the development of the DACP at a more definitive level for the automated system. This document is organized as follows:

INTRODUCTION. The Introduction summarizes the purposes, nature, and organization of the DACP, and includes an explanation of terms.

Section 1. ESTABLISHED CITY POLICY AND CRI-TERIA. This section describes the basic authority and direction for a city-wide data access control program which is fully supported by the Mayor, City Council, and City Manager. A city ordinance has been enacted which creates a Municipal Information Review Board (MIRB) to administer the DACP for the city, define policy for data classification and access, and provide significant related criteria to govern the DACP.

Section 2. ORGANIZATIONAL RESPONSIBILITIES AND PROCEDURES. This section details the organizational and management provisions which are essential to implementing the Data Access Control Plan at the city-wide level. It outlines responsibilities of the city departments, provides for support and coordination by a Municipal Information Office, and describes key mechanisms by which the departments and city management will interact to initiate and maintain an effective program.

Section 3. DATA ACCESS CONTROL FOR THE IMIS. This section provides a comprehensive overview of the security requirements and techniques which are applicable to the system. It identifies the kinds of factors which may cause loss, damage, or compromise of data confidentiality. A feasible means of protecting vulnerable system elements against identified hazards is also discussed. Techniques pertaining to software, data base, remote terminals, personnel, facilities, and the computer are discussed and evaluated in relation to the IMIS program and environment.

Objectives for the Plan are to establish the approach being taken, identify elements of the Plan and document each element as thoroughly as possible. Actually, elements vary in phasing, from those which have been implemented to those which are at a conceptual stage. Because of the complexity and long-term nature of fully implementing the plan, it is anticipated that such a variation will exist for an extended period. This document will be expanded and revised periodically to incorporate the firm planning and/or implementation of individual program elements as they occur.

Explanation of Terms and Abbreviations

Terms and phrases listed below vary according to general usage and are utilized frequently in this plan. The explanations given for terms and phrases are designed to clarify their intended meanings for use in this document, not necessarily to constitute precise definitions.

Classification—"Classification" is the process of placing data into an established category for purposes of controlling data collection, access, or dissemination.
Confidential—This term is used as a general label for any level of data classification which places a limitation on authorized access to the data. In Charlotte, the "confidential" term covers the specific classifications of Restricted and Highly Restricted.
Data Access Control—If no other explanation is given, this term covers the general topic of the DACP. It refers to the control of data for purposes of either protecting against or making positive provisions for access to the data, and covers categorically the various measures (or subtopics) relating to those purposes. However, it does imply direct concern with special controls in matters of public interest, as distinguished from routine or normal controls for general data processing efficiency.
Information—The terms "information" and "data" are used interchangeably in this Plan.
Non-Personal Data—As defined by city ordinance in Charlotte, Non-Personal data are either (1) data which are not concerned with people, or (2) data about persons who are not individually identifiable.
Public Record—This term covers any municipal data classified as "Public" according to criteria established by a city ordinance and interpreted for specific application by the Municipal Information Review Board.

100

Security—This form, as applied to municipal data, is defined as the condition of being safe from loss, damage, or compromise of confidentiality.

Abbreviations used frequently in the Plan are listed and explained below.

DPR—Department of Primary Responsibility. DPR is the designation applied to any department, board, commission, or other municipal agency, which has the primary responsibility for identifying, classifying, and controlling access to specified municipal data. Normally, the DPR is the department responsible for the public function for which given data are collected and maintained. within the city.

IMIS—Integrated Municipal Information System. The IMIS is a computer based information system being designed to provide automated data processing support to operational departments and agencies of the City of Charlotte.

MIS—Municipal Information Office. As a staff office of the MIS Department, the Municipal Information Office supports the MIRB, city departments, and citizens in matters pertaining to the city Data Access Control Program.

MIS Department—Municipal Information System Department. The MIS department is responsible for developing and operating the IMIS.

MIRB—Municipal Information Review Board. A formally constituted body of citizens of the City of Charlotte, the Municipal Information Review Board maintains surveillance and direction of the city's Data Access Control Program.

1. CITY POLICY

Provisions described in this section represent guidance established by city legislation for developing and implementing procedures for data access control in the City of Charlotte.

The need for legislation to provide firm direction for the Data Access Control Program was recognized at an early point in the IMIS Project by officials of the city and other members of the Charlotte Consortium. A draft of the proposed ordinance was developed by the University of North Carolina Institute of Government. This draft was refined through study and coordination with city officials and adopted by action of the City Council in November 1972. *

The ordinance established a new and formally constituted Board within the city government structure having the specific authority to monitor and provide direction to the Data Access Control Plan. In addition, the ordinance defines city policy for classifying municipal information into specific categories for control purposes, defines formal policy governing access procedures, and establishes other significant features for the program which are summarized in the following parts of this section.

1.1 Municipal Information Review Board (MIRB)

The Municipal Information Review Board is the central authority for formulating policy and regulating the collection, storage, use, and dissemination of all municipal information. This board is composed of seven members, whose appointments and terms of service occur as follows:

- Members are appointed by the Mayor, who designates one of the associates to serve as chairman.
- The term of each appointment is normally for a three-year period. Members serve without compensation.
- A given appointee may not serve for more than two three-year periods in succession.
- A staggered appointment schedule will be established and designed to avoid major discontinuities of experience.
- Midterm vacancies, as they occur, will be filled by replacement appointees.
- Appointees and replacements will be selected (a) to maintain a high level of individual competence and integrity and (b) to represent a cross section of citizens and public interests within the city.

Functions of the MIRB are to regulate and supervise the data security and access practices of city departments, boards, commissions, and all other agencies which handle municipal data under the aegis of the city government. The MIRB's authority and responsibilities apply equally to the two major facets of the general access control problem, namely: (a) protecting information privacy and (b) assuring proper access to public records. Its powers and duties include:

- Formulation of municipal data access control policies and recommendations to the City Council concerning regulations

---

*A copy of the ordinance can be found in Appendix A.—Ed.

which should be enacted as ordinances of the city. Such regulations encompass:

The collection of information by municipal departments;
The classification of information into access categories;
The guidelines for storage, use, and dissemination of information in each access category.

- Review and supervision on a continuing basis of the nature and classification of the information that is being collected, stored, used, and disseminated by the city.
- Review and approval of techniques employed by the MIS and other city departments for safeguarding confidential information and for providing ready access to public information.
- Formulation and implementation of procedures for appeals.
- Function as the central decision-making body to resolve matters not clearly covered by existing statutes or other established guidelines pertaining to information classification, protection, or access.

1.2 Classification Policy

Information contained in the municipal data base may be characterized as being either Personal or Non-Personal. Personal data are facts about individual citizens where the individuals are identifiable in relation to the facts. Non-Personal data are either (a) information which is not concerned with people or (b) information about persons where the individuals are not identifiable. These two types of data provide a basis for concepts and policies of data classification.

Classification is the process of placing data into an established category for purposes of governing data collection, access, or dissemination. The categories described below apply to information which is in the municipal system or which may be proposed for collection and storage by municipal departments or agencies.

1.2.1 Public

The Public classification applies to all Non-Personal data. Exceptions occur in cases where (a) a specific statute requires that the information be kept confidential or (b) the municipal agency collecting or producing the information has a compelling public purpose for limiting access to the information and is specifically authorized by the Municipal Information Review Board to classify the information in a higher category.

The Public classification applies to Personal data only in cases where there is a specific statute which requires the information to be maintained as a public record.

1.2.2 Restricted

The Restricted classification applies to all Personal data except in cases where (a) there is a specific statute requiring the information to be maintained as a public record or (b) the municipal agency collecting the information presents to the MIRB a compelling public purpose for denying access to the individual about whom the information is kept and the MIRB specifically authorizes a Highly Restricted classification of the data.

The Restricted classification applies to Non-Personal data only in cases where (a) a specific statute requires that the information be kept confidential or (b) a responsible municipal agency presents a compelling public purpose for limiting access and the Restricted classification is specifically authorized by the MIRB.

1.2.3 Highly Restricted

The Highly Restricted classification applies to sets of data which are specifically so classified by the Municipal Information Review Board. These sets of data will normally consist of Personal data for which compelling purposes have been demonstrated by the responsible municipal agency for denying access to the individual about whom the information is kept. They may also include certain Non-Personal data which is so classified because of a specific statute or for which highly limited access has been shown to be in the public interest.

1.3 Access Policy

A register will be maintained in the Municipal Information System (MIS) Department of all information collected, produced, or stored by the City of Charlotte. The register will set forth the following information in respect to each municipal agency collecting, producing, or storing information:
- Name and location of the agency;
- Agency head, and if there is one, the person designated as record keeper;
- The nature of the information collected, produced, or stored;
- The classification of each type of information;
- The classes of persons and the city agencies for whom access is authorized.

No person authorized to collect or have access to Restricted or Highly Restricted information may give this information to other persons for whom access has not been specifically authorized. Nor may any such authorized person use the information for any purpose other than that purpose for which the MIRB authorized collection or access. Any willful collection, storage, use, or dissemination of municipal information which is contrary to these policies is punishable in accordance with city ordinance.

Appeals from actions by officers and employees of the city in the performance of their duties of collecting, storing, using, or disseminating municipal information will be submitted to the Municipal Information Review Board.

A person about whom information is being collected, stored, used, or disseminated in violation of the ordinance may enjoin the collection, storage, usage, or dissemination of the information by injunction.

The head of the agency that collects or produces information is the custodian of that information. A request for access to public records by any person, or for access to confidential information by an authorized person, is made to the head of the agency that collected or produced the information or by his authorized designee. Access will be controlled by all municipal departments and agencies according to the criteria set forth below:

Public: Information classified as Public will be open for inspection by any person at reasonable times. Any person may obtain certified copies of the data upon payment of reasonable fees as prescribed by the city agency responsible for furnishing copies.

Restricted. Access to Restricted information is normally limited to authorized personnel of the agency responsible for the public function for which the information is collected and maintained. Access to this information by other persons or agencies will be controlled as follows:

- Any city department that requires access to municipal information placed in the Restricted category that was collected or produced by another department or agency of the city, and any non-city governmental agency that wants access to municipal information placed in the Restricted category, is required to have such access approved by the Municipal Information Review Board. The Board may approve access if the agency seeking access has a proper governmental purpose in inspecting the information.
- Any person not acting in the performance of duties as a municipal employee, other than an individual seeking access to information about himself, that wants access

to Restricted information is required to have such access approved by the MIRB. The Board may approve access if the person seeking access has a compelling public purpose for inspecting the information.

● Every person has the right of access to any information pertaining directly to him which is maintained in the Restricted access category. Every person has the right to add to or correct any such record pertaining to him upon the presentation of identification and proof of the correction to the municipal agency collecting or producing the record.

Highly Restricted. Information in the Highly Restricted category is open only to those authorized personnel of the agency responsible for performing the public function for which the information is collected or produced and maintained.

2. ORGANIZATIONAL RESPONSIBILITIES AND PROCEDURES

To implement the concepts and policies described in the preceding section, it is necessary to establish and assign responsibilities to city departments and to provide feasible working mechanisms by which the departments relate to each other and to the Municipal Information Review Board. This section addresses those areas, emphasizing the management structure and procedures which provide essential prerequisites for dealing with the technical aspects of data control and access.

2.1   City Department Responsibilities

According to terms of the city ordinance, the requirements for positive action are placed on all city departments and other agencies which are under management control of the Mayor, City Council, and/or the City Manager. Specifically, the ordinance states that:

"The head of the department, agency, board or commission* that collects or produces information is the

---

*A "department, agency, board or commission" is referred to herein as a "department" which handles municipal information and operates within the authority of the city management.

custodian of that information. A request for access to
public records by any person or for access to restricted
information by an approved person shall be made to the
custodian or his designee. The custodian or his designee
shall grant access to any person entitled to access under
this ordinance."

A list has been compiled and coordinated to identify by name
the organizations or specific organizational units, and their heads,
who will be recognized formally by the MIRB as responsible for complying with requirements of the city ordinance and this Plan.* The
list is updated to reflect organizational changes as they occur.

The provisions which are being made within the IMIS Project
for data sharing by departments and for the centralized storage and
processing of data require a specific definition of the meaning of
"custodian" as referred to in the ordinance. The term "Department
of Primary Responsibility (DPR)" has been adopted for this purpose.

The DPR is the department which is responsible for the municipal function for which a given set of information is collected and utilized. The information may be stored and used or disseminated by
that department, manually or otherwise, or it may be computerized
for storage and processing by the centralized IMIS. However, this
responsibility may become ambiguous in some areas as increasing
amounts of data are introduced into the IMIS, and as improved techniques evolve for common uses of municipal data by authorized departments and persons. It may be necessary for the MIRB to designate
one department as the DPR for a given data, on arbitrary grounds,
and/or to designate the MIS Department as the DPR for specified data.

For these reasons, the DPR is defined as the department which
is recognized by the MIRB, specifically with respect to each identified
set of municipal data. Correspondence with a department's established
public function will continue to be the primary criterion. The need
for the DPR concept and its implications are further indicated in
discussions of responsibilities and procedures in the following parts
of this section.

As approved and amplified by the MIRB, individual departments
will be charged with the following responsibilities for municipal data
classification and access control:

- Classification of all municipal data collected by the department in accordance with the established city ordinance,
  other applicable statutes, MIRB directives, and the Data
  Access Control Plan.

---

*See Appendix B.—Ed.

- All necessary action to insure that (1) free access to public records is provided to the public at all reasonable times and (2) access to confidential information is provided to, and only to, authorized persons in accordance with established policy.
- Implementation of all necessary security measures to protect municipal data according to the type and classification of the data collected, stored, used, or disseminated by the department. Security measures will encompass protection against loss, damage, or compromise of confidentiality, whether by deliberate action or accidental means.
- Implementation of procedures for preparing and presenting to the MIRB proposals, requests, or reports associated with data classification and access that are set forth in the Data Access Control Plan.

Responsibilities for adequate protection of confidential data by each department apply equally to all data to which the department has authorized access and to data for which the department is the DPR.

The department which is recognized as the DPR for identified data may authorize the MIS Department or in special cases, another city department which uses the data for related functions to act as its agent for purposes of providing access to the data by the public and by authorized persons in accordance with established policy. Each such authorization will be approved by the MIRB for the given data, and the agency designated for access will be identified in the Municipal Information Register. Normally, the designating department will continue to be identified as the DPR for the data.

The responsibilities described above apply to the MIS Department as well as to others. In addition to being DPR for some data, it is anticipated that the MIS Department will become the designated access agent for other departments as larger amounts of municipal data are stored and handled by the IMIS. Because of this key role, and the scope and volumes of data to be involved in its operations, actions of the MIS Department to implement security and the positive measures necessary to comply with the access requirements will need significant attention.

In addition, the MIS Department is charged by city ordinance with the function of providing staff support to the MIRB. This staff support role is viewed as a key function in the city's entire information security and access management structure. To perform the function adequately, the MIS Department established a special staff office, known as the Municipal Information Office, which is further described below.

2.2 Municipal Information Office (MIO)

The MIO is organized as a staff office which reports directly to the MIS Department Manager. It performs functions in support of the MIRB and other city departments to assure effective management of matters pertaining to municipal data security and access. The responsibilities of the MIO include the following:

- To provide administrative support to the MIRB by issuing agenda and taking minutes, processing proposals for data classification and requests for access, maintaining files of MIRB administrative data, and preparing and distributing MIRB action documents.
- To provide technical staff analysis support to the MIRB by conducting, as required, staff studies of classification proposals, access requests, or other action items for presentation to the Board, in order to identify the relevant technical or municipal impact of potential decisions by the Board.
- To monitor security and access procedures and provisions of all municipal departments; to provide security support to departments by disseminating information relating to such matters as MIRB policy, security methods, and training; to monitor status of municipal security and access provisions; to report status and requirements to the Board.
- To maintain this Data Access Control Plan by periodic updating to incorporate revisions and expansions based on evolving MIRB policy, study, and operating experience of the municipal departments.
- To establish and maintain a central municipal data access information service by compiling and maintaining the Municipal Information Register and by providing an information service to assist the public, city departments, and other agencies or persons in matters pertaining to municipal data access.

With regard to the last-mentioned area, it is not anticipated that the MIO will provide access to municipal information on any broad scale. A capability will be developed, in time, as a line function of MIS Department data processing operations to provide such a service. Inherent in its function, however, the MIO will serve as the DPR relating to the city's data security and access system as a whole. It is recognized that actions of the MIRB and the documentation of those actions are matters of public record which will be of interest to many agencies and persons, both within and external to the city.

2.3 Municipal Information Review Board (MIRB)

The responsibilities of the MIRB are listed in section 1.1. Formal functions of the Board are performed in the course of periodic or special meetings. Regularly scheduled meetings occur at quarterly intervals. These can be supplemented by special interim meetings as requested by the Mayor or City Council, and as the Board considers necessary to handle its workload.

Board meetings and actions are governed by accepted rules of procedure for similar public bodies, to include the following:

- Any meeting of the Board at which a quorum is present; and which results in any official Board action, will be a public meeting. Time, place, and agenda for the meeting are announced to the public in advance, and the meeting is held at a place suitable for public attendance.
- A simple majority (four) constitutes a quorum for the purpose of conducting an official meeting.
- Decisions are determined by vote. Agreement by a simple majority of members present at an official meeting is sufficient to reach a decision.
- As approved by the chairman, individuals representing themselves or any agency may be invited to participate in a Board meeting for purposes of presenting information, or answering questions, pertaining to an agenda item.

Succeeding parts of this section are devoted to identifying major initial types of data access control actions with which the Board is concerned, and the manner in which the Board, the MIO, city departments, and others interact to accomplish those actions. Figure 1 illustrates the organizational setting in which the procedures apply.

In the control actions discussed below, the MIRB is depicted principally in its role as a decision-making body. It is expected that important portions of the Board's time will also be devoted to reviews, supervision, and related functions outlined in the preceding section. Above all, it is evident that continuing attention will be required to refine the principles and criteria which apply to questions of privacy and access, since those are the ingredients that must be supplied by the MIRB in order for the procedures to work effectively in the public interest.

2.4 Procedures

Formal procedures for classifying sets of municipal data and controlling data access will be implemented gradually, with the long-term objective that procedures encompass all significant data handled by the city departments, whether in manual or automated form.

FIGURE 1
CITY OF CHARLOTTE ORGANIZATION
FOR MUNICIPAL DATA ACCESS CONTROL

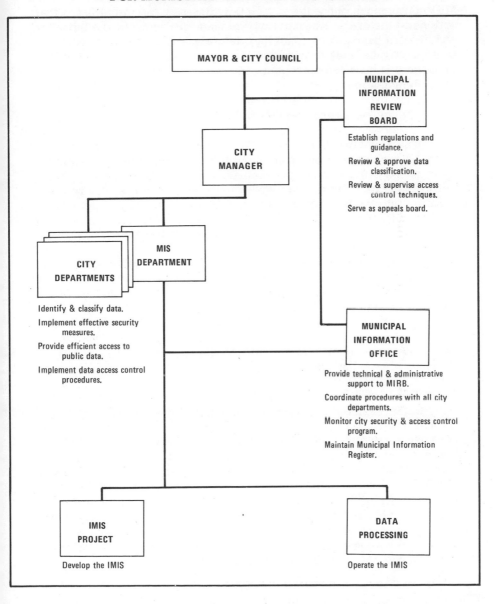

The following subsections outline the manner in which certain key proposals, notifications, or requests are to be initiated by city departments, or others, and how these actions are processed through MIO management support and MIRB decisions. It is anticipated that actions in the areas described will account for much of the initial and ongoing business of municipal data classification and access control. Hence, they provide the basis for expanded planning to include additional related areas as the program moves into active stages of implementation.

2.4.1 Municipal Information Register

The Municipal Information Register serves as the vehicle for documenting information. The Register is initiated by the Municipal Information Office at the time the MIO is sufficiently staffed. The initial issue includes all data which have been identified for incorporation into the IMIS and a limited sample of other municipal data. Subsequent issues are expanded to include new IMIS data as they are identified, and to include additional descriptions of manual data which are input by the city departments.

Listings of data contained in the Register consists of titles expressed in lay language, or in established terminology of the DPR, together with descriptions which identify the scope and nature of the data referred to by each entry. Additionally, the classification and access information is identified for each entry as required by the city ordinance (see 1.3) and is further described below. The MIO is responsible for developing an index to the Register and such other guidance data as may be necessary to support its efficient use as an authoritative reference document.

The level at which sets of data are aggregated into single entries in the Register will vary depending on the type of data, its normal uses, and other factors. In general, an entry should encompass elements of data which are normally accessed and used as a set, and should be confined to data which are the responsibility of a single department. The determinations are expected to become complex in some cases. In the process of developing the Register, and in the course of its use, the MIO will develop rules and criteria to guide the DPRs in formulating and inputting their entries. As indicated below, these entries are important to the mechanics of data access control, throughout, since they serve as the units of municipal information upon which the MIRB takes its various actions.

2.4.2 Municipal Information Identification

As indicated above, it is necessary to separate municipal information as a whole into subsets of data for purposes of listing in the Municipal Information Register, and there are reasons to use these same subsets as the recognized units for other aspects of data access control. To distinguish these subsets of data from various other ways in which data are grouped within the municipality—e.g., as manual or automated files, records, segments, reports, or other— each grouping is referred to as a Municipal Information Register Entry, or more simple, as a Register Entry.

A Register Entry must be related to the organization of data files within the city, including the IMIS, although there are reasons why direct correspondence will not occur in many cases. The relationships must be determined during the course of identifying Register Entries, and of structuring or restructuring actual municipal data files, and must be known by each DPR or authorized designee for purposes of permitting inspection and providing copies of the data covered by an established Register when required.

Register Entries are to be identified by each city department and described on a standard form issued by the Municipal Information Office. The form, the Register Entry Identification Form, is accompanied by detailed instructions and guidance for its preparation, and requires the following types of information relating to each entry.

- Name and location of the department (DPR)
- Name and signature of the department head
- Name, signature, and department affiliation (if different) of the individual responsible for preparing the form
- Identification of the data as Personal or Non-Personal
- Title of the proposed Register Entry
- A description and accurate summary of the data referred to by the given title, including identification of significant elements or subsets of data covered by the entry
- Justification of the proposed classification, if not obvious; a justification is normally required in cases where:
  (1) A Public or Highly Restricted classification is proposed for Personal data; and
  (2) A Restricted or Highly Restricted classification is proposed for Non-Personal data
- Information relating to access for purposes of inspection only, e.g.: form of storage; location; contact person or office; required arrangements or limitations for authorized access, if any
- Information relating to copies of the data, e.g.: whether available; where; cost, time, or other limitations of availability.
- Recommended other departments or persons authorized access to the data on a periodic or demand basis (applicable to confidential entries only), to include applicable restrictions

113

pertaining to specific individuals, specific uses, and/or dissemination

- Recommended other department authorized as designee for providing access to ad hoc requesters, and/or for supplying copies.

In addition to the basic information outlined above, the form includes spaces for use by the MIO to record events during its subsequent processing. Some of the information on the form is for the purpose of providing an adequate basis for MIRB approval. Selected portions of the total are subsequently used by the MIO in composing the Register Entry.

The total task of initiating and processing Register Entry Identifications for the full spectrum of municipal information will be one of considerable magnitude. For this reason, the task is initiated and completed in increments. To take advantage of the IMIS Project resources and developmental orientation, it begins with those departments that are identified as users of the IMIS and with the sets of data that are now, or are scheduled to become, automated. Schedules for completing Register Entry Identifications for these automated data correspond with schedules for the Module Design Specifications which reference and define the affected data.

Requirements and instructions for additional coverage are disseminated to all departments during the initial phase, and schedules for inputting the identifications are developed for the departments on an individual basis.

Completed Register Entry Identifications are submitted by DPRs to the MIO for review, correlation, and presentation to the MIRB for approval of classifications and access authorizations. Approval of Register Entry Identifications by the MIRB are documented by means of MIRB directives. The MIO establishes and maintains a file of all MIRB directives and distributes action copies of each directive to the affected departments. In addition, the MIO composes a Register Entry based on each approved identification, coordinates it with the DPR, and incorporates the Entry into the Register.

Actions taken by the MIRB relating to proposed Register Entry Identifications may include approval, disapproval, or deferment for corrections/revisions or further study. A disapproval action may result if the Board decides that proposed data are not required by a given department to perform its legitimate public function, or are not suitable for collection and storage by any city agency.

Implementing actions by DPRs, authorized designees, and departments authorized access to other departments' data are to be taken as necessary and appropriate to the given data and department. As the program develops, individual departments will be required by the MIRB to document their internal data identification/classification

114

procedures. Departments may be asked to present summaries of implementation status, accomplishments, or problems and recommendations at Board meetings.

Those departments that are users of the IMIS, or scheduled to become users, will normally be assisted by members of an IMIS Project analysis and design team in preparing the initial Register Entry Identifications, in conjunction with developing the associated Module Design Specifications. When approved by the MIRB, the data classification and access provisions are also appropriately specified for each Process in the Module Design Specifications. In this form— i.e., as firm requirements set forth in the specifications—the provisions serve as governing criteria for the subsequent development of software, data file organization, and other measures associated with access and security of the given data within the IMIS.

Early and continuing emphasis is placed on this initial step of identifying the municipal information which exists, systematically throughout the city and on defining the classification and access provisions which apply to each identified part of the total.

2.4.3   Register Entry Changes

Once processed and approved for listing in the Municipal Information Register, the Register Entries are subject to change resulting from any of a variety of causes—c.g., relating to the titles, nature and uses of the data, retirement, classification, access authorizations, or any other of the elements contained in each entry. Currency and accuracy of its contents are recognized as essential for tho Register to meet requirements which are specified by city ordinance.

It is the responsibility of each department to both incorporate routine internal procedures for notifying the MIO whenever an entry is affected by events and to conduct periodic reviews of the entries listed in the Register for which it is the DPR. As custodian of the Register, and in the course of its normal use and maintenance, the MIO provides continuing support to the departments in identifying needed changes. To facilitate preparation of change notifications and requests by DPRs, the MIO issues standard change initiation forms to all departments and implements routine procedures for processing and implementing the changes in the Register. Forms and procedures are governed by the guidelines outlined below:

- Register Entry Change 'Request. Any proposed change to classification or to access authorizations will be documented by the DPR as a Register Entry Change Request and submitted to the MIO. These require MIRB approval prior to being incorporated into the Register.

- Register Entry Change Notification. All other changes which affect the content or intent of a Register Entry are documented by the DPR as a Register Entry Change Notification and submitted to the MIO. These do not require MIRB approval, but are subject to MIRB review and concurrence at the Board's discretion.

The MIO accomplishes minor editorial and format changes as a normal part of preparing and maintaining the Register. These need not be separately documented but are subject to review and concurrence by the DPR.

Information required on forms for submitting Requests and Notifications is similar. A single form serves both purposes, with a space to check indicating whether it is one or the other. Any Register Entry Change Request, for example, should also report other changes to the entry which may accompany a proposed change in classification or access. The required information will always consist, basically, of a precise description of the proposed change(s) to the entry. In addition, it should contain such items as the following:

- Relevant explanatory statements or references which may be useful for record purposes.
- Full identification of any known impacts of the change on other departments or agencies/persons external to the city government and, where relevant, a statement of the status of coordination with those other departments or agencies.
- Justification of proposed changes in classification or access authorizations, in sufficient detail to provide a basis for MIRB decision.
- Identifying and administrative data associated with the change, e.g., department name, date of preparation, authorizing signatures and dates.

The Register Entry Change Notification is issued to delete an entry from the Register when data are retired or purged from the DPRs files. It is not used to completely replace an old entry with a new one. In the case of major changes in the nature and content of data covered by an entry, the MIO may advise deletion and replacement via Register Entry Identification rather than through change action.

The initial Register Entry Identifications, Register Entry Change Requests, and Register Entry Change Notifications must always represent official actions of the recognized DPRs for individual entries. They may not be issued by any other department or agency, although the MIO, MIS Department, and others may recommend the change to the DPR or assist in its documentation. Disagreements with DPR decisions may be referred to the MIO for arbitration or appeal to the MIRB, or may result in other actions outside MIRB jurisdiction, e.g., injunction, as appropriate to the disagreement and circumstances.

Within the IMIS Project, all changes to the Module Design Specifications, following their initial completion and approvals, are controlled by the IMIS Design Review Board. Procedures employed in processing changes to the specifications incorporate routine provisions for examining each proposed change for potential impact on the established security and access requirements. When those requirements are affected, such changes also require notification of the DPR, preparation by the DPR of a Register Entry Change Request, and approval by the MIRB prior to being implemented in the IMIS. Conversely, MIO procedures incorporate routine provisions for notifying the IMIS Design Review Board of all changes originated independently by DPRs which affect software or other IMIS elements and procedures.*

2.4.4 Ad Hoc Access Requests

Each DPR is responsible for providing public access to all of that department's information which carries a Public classification. By city ordinance, each department is to keep Public data open for inspection by any person at reasonable times, and arrange for providing certified copies upon payment of a reasonable fee. Departments are individually responsible for developing efficient practices in handling requests, providing requested access and copies, and keeping such records of public access as they deem necessary, except as specific measures may be directed by the MIRB to correct reported deficiencies.

In volume, Public data constitute the bulk of information which is handled by the average department and which is made available for use by other agencies and persons external to the DPR. Capabilities of the IMIS to provide efficient response to ad hoc requests for Public data receive continuing emphasis as an inherent objective of the IMIS development program.

The procedures discussed below are limited to ad hoc requests for access to confidential data—i.e., to those which carry a Restricted

---

*Implementing data access control in the IMIS will be facilitated in many of its aspects by the established IMIS procedures for maintaining firm control of system documents, procedures, and changes thereto. A description of the specification practices and change control system for IMIS is contained in the System Design Guide, MIS-3201/000.

or Highly Restricted classification. The Municipal Information Register identifies specific departments or persons who have been recommended by the DPR and authorized by the MIRB for access to identified sets of confidential data on a regular basis, or as needed. The term "ad hoc" is used to distinguish those requests that are made on occasion for access to confidential data by persons or agencies who are not specifically identified in the Register as being authorized for access to the data in question. This category of requests includes both those which the DPR may authorize individually in compliance with established statutes and MIRB policy, and those which must be referred to the MIRB for specific decisions.

It is the city's policy to require that each ad hoc request for access to confidential data be documented, and that adequate records be maintained for a reasonable period of time of all such requests and their disposition. The MIO will provide the necessary standard forms for this purpose. The form(s) are to be employed by the requester, the DPR, MIO, and MIRB, as appropriate to the type of request, to record information such as the following:

- Name, agency affiliation, and signature of the applicant.
- Identification of the Register Entry covering data to which the access is requested, or comparable identification if the Register Entry is not yet established; where applicable, identification of the specific elements or data subset.
- Reasons and proposed uses of the data.
- Authority for permitting access (by DRB)—e.g., citing specific statute or MIRB directive.
- Data pertaining to access, when permitted; e.g., date and time(s); whether inspection only or copies; identification of specific copies and content provided.
- Affirmation of the applicant, as appropriate, to prevent further disclosure.
- Administrative data; e.g., DPR identification; date of request and approval; authorizing signatures and dates.

An example of the Request for Confidential Data Form is given in Figure 2. Under terms of the existing city ordinance, each request must be addressed to the DPR, or to his authorized designee. Inquiries made to other agencies will be so referred, except for requests addressed to the MIO which clearly require MIRB consideration. In these cases the MIO will initiate the request and obtain the DPR's recommendations.

DPRs document each request and associated information as appropriate to the given case, and normally honor requests which are authorized by established statute or policy; e.g., as for individuals requesting access to Restricted information about themselves. DPRs retain records of requests and the actions taken, and in addition,

FIGURE 2
MUNICIPAL INFORMATION SYSTEM
REQUEST FOR CONFIDENTIAL DATA

MUNICIPAL INFORMATION SYSTEM REQUEST FOR CONFIDENTIAL DATA	NO:	DATE:
	NAME OF REQUESTER:	
	AGENCY:	

REQUESTED DATA:

REASON FOR REQUEST AND PROPOSED USE OF DATA (INCLUDE NAMES OF ALL PERSONS TO BE GRANTED ACCESS):

ACCESS REQUIREMENT:

☐ INSPECTION ONLY   ☐ COPY   NO. COPIES REQ'D _____

ACCESS DURATION:

☐ SINGLE   ☐ PERMANENT   ☐ FROM   __ __/__ __/__ __ TO __ __/__ __/__ __

The undersigned affirms that the data requested will be used only for the purposes so stated and will be safeguarded from disclosure to persons other than those indicated above.

SIGNATURE OF REQUESTER: _____

THE SPACE BELOW IS INTENDED FOR USE BY MUNICIPAL INFORMATION OFFICE PERSONNEL ONLY.

☐ REQUEST DENIED   ☐ REQUEST APPROVED   ☐ COPY CONTROL NO(S). _____

AUTHORIZING SIGNATURE: _____ DATE: _____

RELEASE AUTHORITY: _____

copies are furnished periodically; e.g., weekly, to the MIO. The MIO uses these records for monitoring the access request activities and for preparing such summary reports as may be directed by the MIRB.

Any request which the DPR is not clearly authorized to honor will be referred to the MIO, with the DPRs' recommendations when indicated, for screening and subsequent submission of valid requests to the MIRB. Valid includes any request which the requester insists upon pursuing and which is not clearly ruled out by law. The MIO conducts necessary staff studies of each request and presents its analysis and recommendations, together with those of the DPR, to support consideration of the request by the Board.

3. DATA ACCESS CONTROL FOR THE IMIS

This section addresses procedures in the Integrated Municipal Information System (IMIS) necessary to control data access in accordance with policies governing the protection and dissemination of municipal information which have been established by the City of Charlotte. The section also outlines the scope and nature of the problem, and documents the level at which the Planning has been developed for individual elements of data access control as they apply to the automated system. An organized set of basic material is provided which can be expanded and refined progressively in the course of continued analysis planning and implementation.

The Plan emphasizes factors associated with maintaining the security of data handled in the IMIS. Data security encompasses the protection of data from loss, modification, or unauthorized disclosure through accidental or deliberate means. Accordingly, this section identifies the classes of hazards or threats to be recognized, and outlines the ways in which the system can be protected against the identified hazards. Feasible countermeasures are discussed as they pertain to personnel, facilities, hardware, software, data base design, and combinations of these, taking into account the IMIS capabilities and operating environment.

The basic problem of data access control is to devise a means of assuring privacy in a multi-user, multi-programming, batch, and on-line remote terminal system environment in which data of different classification categories may be processed simultaneously. In such an environment, the system must permit personnel possessing different access privileges to make use of or operate equipment without compromising any part of the total data base, either by unauthorized access or, just as damaging, by unauthorized entry or deletion of data which will affect decisions made by authorized personnel. It is helpful to make a distinction between these two types of violations, since security measures that reduce the probability of one type of violation do not necessarily reduce that of the other.

A centralized data base facilitates the creation of composite records of individuals. The same is true for Non-Personal data. These records may be the products of independent and often unrelated data inputs to serve specific needs. Aggregations of data other than those specifically authorized must be guarded against. The digital data base will eventually contain quantities of these data, both sensitive and nonsensitive. Any disks, drums, or tapes used in the system will be exposed to this data base; the core memory of the computer will be similarly exposed.

Information leakage in the IMIS can occur in several areas. With regard to hardware, the circuits for protection, such as bounds registers, memory read-write protect, or privileged mode instructions, might fail, thus permitting information to leak to improper destinations. A large variety of hardware failures might contribute to software failures which, in turn, lead to divulgence. Failure of the software may disable such protective features as access control, user identification, or memory bounds control, leading to improper routing of information. Overall, the most serious threat to data security lies in the misuse of information by personnel directly engaged in the management, design, development, implementation, operation, and maintenance of the system. These personnel have the greatest opportunity and skill in gaining access to the data base for purposes of unauthorized disclosure, modification, and destruction. At the same time, any of these personnel could, through carelessness, inattentiveness, or inadequate training, cause the accidental disclosure, modification, or destruction of information in the data base. Consequently, the integrity and experience of system personnel represent critical elements in maintaining data security.

3.1 General Considerations and Policy

The collection, processing, and dissemination of data through the IMIS takes place within the framework of the city policies and procedures for municipal data access control. This section addresses some implications of that framework for the IMIS, and sets forth general policy guidelines to provide a basis for developing and implementing security techniques.

The city requires that departments classify data into access categories, according to specified criteria that apply to Personal and Non-Personal data. The established categories are: Public, Restricted, and Highly Restricted. It is the further responsibility of each department to define access requirements and limitations as they apply to personnel and functions within the given department, and to implement procedures which ensure compliance with those requirements.

The MIS Department has the unique purpose, within the city, of providing automated data processing support to the other operating city departments. In general, such support encompasses a wide range of data handling functions, including collection, conversion to machine-readable form, temporary or permanent storage, data transformations, retrieval for display or printing, dissemination, and destruction. Many of these functions imply that personnel of the IMIS Project and/ or IMIS Data Processing must have access to the data in the course of performing their duties. While this situation creates no unusual problem in the case of Public data, it does pose questions which must be faced and resolved with respect to data which are classified as confidential, and for which some other city department has been designated as the Department of Primary Responsibility (DPR).

In this context, it is useful to distinguish levels and types of access which may be authorized and monitored, and which may apply to system users as well as to the IMIS personnel. Access levels, as they pertain specifically to the system data base and to identified portions thereof, are as follows:

- Non-Access. This level refers to the absence of authorized access to the system data base. (Note: Access to the computer may be authorized independently of access to actual data values contained in the data base.)
- Read Access. A user of the computer or a terminal may be permitted access to specified portions of the system data base for purposes of retrieval only.
- Read-Write Access. This level permits the authorized person not only to retrieve, but to add, modify, or delete data contained in a specified file or segment of a file.

In addition to the above, a Special Access requirement is recognized and assigned to the System Administrator at the central computer facility. This level refers primarily to access to the special tables and/or files containing security control parameters, e.g., passwords. It does not imply authorized access to confidential data which may be contained in user segments or files of the system data base.

In this Plan, and at the current stage of the IMIS development, the security techniques discussed in subsequent sections represent ones which will require time to implement and test. Additionally, questions of cost-benefit must be examined at each step in the specific context of objectives and functions of the IMIS as a whole. Maintaining effective security of confidential data in a system which is basically designed to create a free and efficient exchange of municipal information can be costly, not only in dollars but in potentially negative effects on handling the other data. Hence, the IMIS does not presently have the capabilities to protect all levels of data in full compliance with the city's criteria, and the process of acquiring capabilities that are truly adequate will be a lengthy one.

The policies outlined below are based on the above considerations. They will apply until revised or expanded in subsequent issues of this Plan.

- Restricted data will be stored and processed in the IMIS only to the extent that access can be adequately controlled in compliance with access authorizations specified for the given data in the Municipal Information Register. Introduction of given Restricted data into the IMIS will occur only upon request by the DPR and approval by the MIRB, following verification that protective measures are fully adequate for the purpose.

- The Highly Restricted category does not provide for access to the data by any personnel other than those of the DPR. Data in this category will not be introduced into the IMIS until it can be demonstrated that security measures are adequate to preclude either accidental disclosure or deliberate invasion, including possible disclosure to or invasion by MIS Department personnel.

- Authorized access is always for specifically designated data or subsets of the data contained in the system data base. An access level authorized for specified data is not automatically transferable to other data. Further, no access level including that to Public data, will be recognized which permits read-write access to the system data base as a whole by any one individual Security measures will be designed to eliminate any reasonable possibility that such access can occur.

- Read-write access is normally limited to the DPR for given data, whatever its classification. While files are designed by IMIS personnel, actual data values will be inserted and maintained by each DPR or his authorized designee. The designee may normally be a member of the IMIS staff for data classified as Public which are inserted and maintained at the central computer facility.

3.2   System Security Requirements

This section outlines the capabilities that could be applied in the IMIS to provide adequate security. The capabilities reflect, where applicable, the data classification and access level guidelines

123

discussed in the preceding section. A major subsection is devoted
to each of the topics listed below:
- Personnel Security
- Physical Security
- Hardware Security
- Software Security
- Data Handling & Accountability
- Emergency Procedures

3.2.1 Personnel Security

All persons authorized access to the IMIS are subject to one
or more of the following provisions, commensurate with their re-
sponsibilities. This includes persons authorized as users, system
personnel, system managers, and personnel responsible for building
maintenance and equipment maintenance.
- Bonding by a national insurance company
- Signing of an affidavit or non-disclosure employment con-
tract
- Background investigation
- Periodic security indoctrination
- Thorough training in operating and administrative procedures
- Data and access level restrictions on a need-to-know basis

Administration of the foregoing provisions is the assigned responsibility of a Security Officer designated by the System Administrator.

3.2.1.1 Training

Manuals, films, and slides are developed to indoctrinate users
and system personnel thoroughly in system security at the time they
begin working in the system and at periodic intervals thereafter.
This training accomplishes the following:
- Explains the data classification and access level classification scheme used in the city and in the system. Also explains the importance of maintaining the trust and confidence
of citizens in handling sensitive data concerning individuals.
- Makes personnel aware of present laws or anticipated legislation in the municipality which provide penalties for an
employee's actions in failing to safeguard the security of
information which is in his custody or to which he may have
access.
- Alerts personnel to report the presence of unauthorized
individuals at the computer and terminal facilities, and to
report any apparent violations of system security that come
to their attention.

- Explains the formal procedures governing the handling of confidential data and physical access to the computer facility, equipment, and data base media.

3.2.2   Physical Security

3.2.2.1   Fire Protection

The following provisions are required to protect the system against potential damage or loss by fire:
- Computer facilities are constructed of fireproof materials throughout, including partitions, floor, built-in storage, and paint.
- Good housekeeping practices are enforced; e.g., no waste paper or carbons on the floor.
- Smoking inside the computer room is restricted, where necessary, to reduce fire hazards or to prevent contaminating media such as tapes.
- Fire extinguishers installed are types that minimize damage to equipment or data files (e.g., CO_2 or Halon extinguishing agents).
- Smoke, temperature deviation, and humidity detectors are installed which will actuate calls, automatically, to designated telephones in the event of emergency.
- File media is stored in fireproof containers.

3.2.2.2   Power Protection

Protection against power blackout or brownout is achieved by using multiple external power sources and/or by installation of an independent standby power supply unit.

3.2.2.3   Air Conditioning Protection

The operation of a computer depends heavily on closely controlled temperature and humidity. An air conditioning unit with sufficient capacity to do the job must be maintained in peak operating condition. Additionally, arrangements are made to divert air conditioning equipment serving other parts of the building to the computer room in case of emergency.

3.2.2.4   Facility Location

Within the building, the computer center is located out of the main traffic stream, out of public view, and behind substantial walls. It is not situated to attract uninvited attention.

3.2.2.5 Facility Access

Access to and exit from the computer center is restricted by electrically operated doors. Access through the doors by card key or, from the inside, by a receptionist. Only known or properly escorted persons are admitted. Badges bear photographs for positive identification and are coded to denote the areas within the facility to which an individual has authorized access.

Remote terminals are provided with locks to prevent unauthorized operation. In addition, the terminals normally are located in rooms secured by locks and/or guards.

3.2.2.6 Insurance

Insurance provides added protection to cover equipment damage or destruction, data base media loss, and expenses resulting from the interruption of operations. Insurance costs for EDP equipment are generally substantial because of the high concentration of value in a relatively small area. However, costs are reduced when it can be demonstrated that the facility is provided with effective fire protection, backup air conditioning units, building access, and personnel safeguards.

3.2.2.7 Contingency Operations

Provisions are made for contingency operations in the event of damage or destruction of IMIS equipment. Essential operations (e.g., payroll) are identified and formal arrangements are made with another compatible computer facility to conduct those operations. Backup copies of computer programs and data base segments required for those essential operations are stored in a location physically removed from the facility used for normal operations. To assure that the identified contingency operations can be performed at the alternate facility, test operations are performed prior to acceptance of the facility and at scheduled intervals thereafter.

3.2.3 Hardware Security

3.2.3.1 Environmental Considerations

The classification of the computer complex remains fixed and is the highest classification associated with the data to be processed. The complex may itself be divided into smaller units, but the logical, functional result can be considered as a single computer complex in one location. Around this centralized computer complex are various peripheral input/output work stations which have varying security classifications. The security classification of any one station can change with time and may vary over the entire range.

3.2.3.2 Processor

The processor has basic arithmetic and control capability and operates on words or characters. The processor must have more than one mode of operation, must contain a set of privileged instructions which can be operated only when in a control mode, and must contain memory bounds registers to restrict user program access.

Processor Operating Modes. The processor must have two modes of operation, control and user, differing in the ability to process available instructions and in memory access restrictions. In the control mode, the full set of instructions is available and includes unrestricted instructions and privileged instructions.

User programs are executed in the user mode. In this mode, only the unrestricted subset of available instructions can be executed. Any requirement for a function performed by a privileged instruction is fulfilled by a call on the operating system executive, which operates in the control mode. Upon completion of the privileged instruction, and any subsequent executive tasks, control will be restored to some user's job (possibly different from the one which caused the interrupt) and the processor is returned to the user mode.

Interrupts. An interrupt results from one of many possible conditions arising either internally or externally to the processor. An interrupt sets a specific condition bit in an interrupt register. Interrupts may be masked in order to control the priority of servicing, to select which processor performs the servicing, and to allow completion of processing one interrupt without being further interrupted. Interrupt conditions which are required at this time are:

- External input/output activity requests
- Abnormal arithmetic or logical conditions (e.g., overflow)
- Memory bounds violation
- Power failure
- Equipment errors
- Occurrence of a privileged instruction while in user mode
- Real-time clock updating
- Interprocessor communication (if more than one processor)

Flag Bits. Flag bits are contained in memory words which are used for control purposes rather than actual user processing. As such, they are not alterable in the user mode.

Parity Bit. A parity bit is required. A single parity bit detects any single (or odd number of) bit error(s) in the work (character or bit group) in which it is included.

Execute-Only Bit. The execute-only flag bit is required to identify the operating system executive and service programs. For the processor to execute any word in such programs, this bit must be set.

Memory-Bounds-Load Bit. A memory-bounds-load flag bit indicates a memory word from which a user's program can access an object and have the memory bounds registers loaded to bound the object. This flag bit is set only in words of a program reference table, and will be set only by the operating system executive. This table will contain both the memory base addresses and memory bounds for all objects which a user program requires.

Privileged Instructions. Privileged instructions are used to establish or alter the overall control by the processor of user jobs. Security control is dependent upon control of privileged instruction execution. The processor must be in the control mode as a condition for execution of privileged instructions. Privileged instructions provide the following capabilities:

- Input/output command descriptor establishment for later use by the input/output control processor to control information transfer
- Flag-bit setting on memory bounds loading information
- Program request table bounds loading
- Interrupt mask register control
- Interrupt response base address loading
- Mode control register resetting to return to user mode.

A privileged instruction occurring in a user program is treated as illegal and results in an interrupt without execution. This interrupt, like any other, results in entry to the control mode to extract its appropriate response (in this case analysis, logging, and recovery or termination of the user program).

Memory Bounds Registers. The principal features of the hardware recommended for checking addresses is a group of memory bounds registers. A memory bounds register pair defines both upper and lower bounds, and also specifies whether the allowed use is execute-only (for a program area), read-only, or both read and write (for a data area).

CRT Terminal Considerations. If a magnetic tape buffering device is used to interface cathode-ray-tube (CRT) displays with teletype units to provide buffering queue for hard-copy capability at CRT remote terminals, it must be actuated at the remote terminal location and not be susceptible to control by the system. However, data set by a user to this buffering device for relay to the teletype printer must always be obliterated by a permanent-magnet erase head as soon as the data are relayed. In this way, sensitive data will not be retained within the CRT-teletype interface device and cannot be read by another individual at a later time.

Communications Protection. System security is subject to compromise through electromagnetic radiation pickup using listening devices from terminals, communication lines, computers, and peripheral equipment. Also, communication lines can be tapped. At the other end of the scale, instances have been reported in which radiation from airport radars has erased information on data base storage media.

It is not clear at this stage that the costs of countering the foregoing threats are justified for the IMIS, particularly since the costs of penetrating the system via wiretaps and electromagnetic radiation pickup may be costly compared to the value of the information obtained. However, a number of countermeasures are possible. These are presented below for consideration and later resolution:

- The computer room peripheral units, terminals, and even the communication lines can be shielded to prevent leakage of electromagnetic radiation. However, shielded communication lines can be tapped; thus they may be feasible only for local hard-wired lines.
- Dedicated communication lines, either in the form of local hard-wired lines or lines leased from a common carrier, can improve security. An intruder cannot gain access merely by dialing in, although wiretaps are still possible.
- A periodic check can be made on communication lines to detect any possible wiretapping. Unusual line noise might also signal the presence of a tap.

- A good cryptographic system substantially reduces the threat against the communications system. The cryptographic system should contain three basic elements: (1) a set of codes that are difficult to interpret; (2) a mechanism for encoding and decoding at each end of the communications channel; and (3) security procedures to protect the code sets and encoding/decoding mechanisms.

3.2.4 Software Security

3.2.4.1 Operating System

The operating system is the key security element in the software package. It provides protection against the operators and the users at remote terminals. The operation system has a set of rules by which it judges all requested actions, and obeys only those requests which conform to the security parameters established for that particular operation. Under no circumstances should the operating system data and code be modified by users.

3.2.4.2 Input/Output Operations

The operating system performs all input/output (I/O) operations. No user program is permitted to utilize any I/O device except via a call to the operating system. The operating system also manages the system clocks and the main consoles.

3.2.4.3 Memory Bounds Protection

The operating system keeps the user programs bounded by read-write memory protect while they are operating. All I/O actions, and any out-of-area reference by user programs, must be via calls to the operating system. This protects information concerning the security levels and authorized users, data base segments, and outputs from access by the using program. Authority to reference random access peripherals must be established by the operating system and all references checked for validity and authority.

3.2.4.4 User Program Violations

If there is a violation of memory bounds or the use of a privileged instruction by a user instruction, the operating system immediately suspends the offending program and makes log entries. It also prohibits further use of the offending program by the user until specifically authorized by a supervisor. The suspension of violating program requests must be complete: if the task has been divided into multiple concurrent operating activities, all such activities must be terminated; if the task has resulted in a chain of requests, all such requests must be removed from the queue. Essentially, there is a complete abort of all parts of the request, necessary to prevent a user program from making multiple tries against the security system.

3.2.4.5   Remote Terminal Security Control

Access to the system from a remote terminal is restricted to those users known to the system as authorized personnel. Each terminal is assigned a data classification and access level. The operating system denies data base accesses other than those specifically authorized to the terminal.

The operating system periodically checks each remote terminal currently in use to determine how long ago the last communication to or from the terminal took place. If a remote terminal has been idle during the previous checking cycle, the system sends a message to that terminal to the effect that it has been idle too long. If no further communications are sent from that terminal, the terminal is automatically signed off and an entry made in the system log. This feature limits the time the system is open to unauthorized use if a user should fail to sign off before physically leaving his remote terminal.

3.2.4.6 Operating System Testing

The operating system must be tested continuously. For example, the memory bounds protection can be expected to fail with some probability. Every user program which conforms with the security safeguards will be expected to run without violating the memory bounds protection and, therefore, the user program itself will not test such a feature. A special program or some part of the monitor must deliberately and periodically violate the memory bounds protection to verify that the memory bounds protection checker is working. This inspires management confidence in the security safeguards.

3.2.4.7   Security When Debugging

A new program is the one most likely to violate security. Although security rules cannot be suspended for debugging or program testing, some concessions can be made. For example, a program in a debugging state can be flagged and, if a violation occurs, the operating system can log it and send a dump of the program to the user rather than notifying the System Administrator terminal.

.2.4.8   Audit Trail Capability

Software is provided which automatically records the following:
- User log-ons and log-offs, including each user's ID and terminal ID.
- Maintenance log-ons and log-offs for whatever purpose, including names of maintenance personnel and the nature of the maintenance.
- Operator-initiated functions, including the name and function. (From the point of view of logs, the operator will be treated as a user.)
- Each attempt by a user or his program to access files or programs for which he is not authorized, including his ID, terminal ID, and program ID.
- Program abort incidents, including program ID, user ID, terminal ID, and time of abort.
- Any special usage of the system, e.g., generation of passwords, changing of data classification, modification of security parameters; or a record of the type of transaction, including the authority or person under whose cognizance the usage is conducted, and the terminal ID.
- Output operations which the system performs at the request of a user, including those which he directs to be sent to a terminal other than the one from which the request was made. Identification of the file accessed, amount of information read out of or written into the file, and the requesting and receiving terminal IDs recorded. Similar information is logged for all input operations which create or destroy files or instructions, or which change file classifications or security parameters.

The log record contains sufficient detail to permit reconstruction of events which indicate an unsuccessful attempt to penetrate the system or which clearly result in a compromise of information or other security violation. For example, repeated unsuccessful attempts to gain access to the system software or to a file reported by the operating software to the System Administrator terminal. The audit trail should enable security personnel to identify the terminal involved, the user (allegedly), the target data or program, and the system reaction. The log is complete enough to permit the System Administrator to monitor system performance on a real-time or periodic basis. The data collected by the system log is also aggregated at intervals to provide performance statistics which indicate the adequacy of existing security safeguards and to develop new or improved procedures and controls.

3.2.4.9   User Entrance to the System

Recognized users are authorized to enter the system, gain access to specified data, and request certain types of information. Any user attempting to enter the system must first identify himself and his location (i.e., the remote terminal he is using), and then authenticate his identification. The identification/authentication steps may be repeated any number of times during operation, e.g., when particularly sensitive information is requested.

3.2.4.10   User and Terminal Identification

Each user and each terminal is assigned a unique identifier. These identifiers are assigned and stored in system tables, in protected memory, by the System Administrator.

3.2.4.11   Authentication

Authentication is the means by which the operating system is assured the individual at a terminal is the one he represents himself to be. User authentication is provided by a password which is changed periodically. Passwords are assigned and entered in system tables, in protected memory, by the System Administrator; they may be one-time or "throw away" passwords but they should not be user-generated.

3.2.4.12   User Security Profile

All legitimate users of the system have profiles stored in a profile table, in a protected area of memory, by the System Administrator. This table contains the legal authentication responses for that user, clearance of user, and need-to-know caveats relating to particular data, actions, outputs, and operations that can be performed on the data.

3.2.4.13   Data Base Security

The IMIS digital data base contains the majority of the information requiring protection in the system. The access, manipulation, and output of information from the data base must be strictly controlled. This control must apply to the user data base and, in particular, to the security control parameters. A feature of the computer which minimizes the possibility of a user deliberately gaining access to data or to another user's program stored in memory is "relative addressing." Through use of relative addressing a system user is unaware of the exact physical memory locations allocated either to his own program and data or to those of any other user currently on the system. These physical locations change frequently and randomly due to the programs and data being transferred in and out of the computer's memory or between different memory locations, as required, to respond to all users currently on the system. Additional capabilities that could be provided include those discussed in the subparagraphs below.

Building Data Bases. The system does not accept information, for either temporary or continued use, without first receiving from the user a declaration of security control parameters about the data, i.e., data classification, access level authorization, and dissemination caveats.

Access Control. The system maintains an identification of data to which each user is authorized access and the authorized access level (see 1.0). If a user attempts to gain unauthorized access or attempts to perform an unauthorized operation on a legitimately accessed data base segment, the system will not execute the action but will make an appropriate entry in the system audit trail log and print a message at the System Administrator's terminal.

Copying of Data Base Images. Only personnel with read-write access authority for the specified data are allowed to create magnetic tape, drum, disk, or punched-card copies of data base images.

User Security Parameters. The creation, storage, maintenance, and access to system tables containing passwords are operations which can be performed only at the System Administrator's terminal. In addition to passwords, the tables contain other security data pertaining to computer programs, the system data base, and actions authorized to users.

Data Base Classification Changes. Changes to data base classifications and access authorizations can be entered only by the System Administrator.

System Response to Initial Access Requests. Immediately after a user requests access to data and the system ascertains his authorization to access it, the system responds with a message informing the user of the classification and restrictions which are assigned to the handling of that data.

<u>Requested Data Base Output</u>. Restricted data stored in the IMIS data base is structured and keyed, along with the associated user programs, so that retrieval queries will result automatically in a display or printout which clearly labels each page of the output with (a) the classification and (b) any special caveats that apply to the handling of the given data content.

<u>Classified Residue</u>. Classified residue is sensitive information, either code or data, which is left behind in the computer memory after the program that referenced it has been dismissed, swapped out, or quit from the system.

The operating system assures, to the extent it is technically feasible, that no sensitive data can remain as accessible residue in either primary or secondary storage. The classification residue problem pertains to all forms of secondary storage, e.g., drums, tapes, or disks, as well as to the primary core store.

The standard solution to classification residue is to purge the contaminated memory dynamically, for example by overwriting with random numbers or zeros. This solution is prohibitively expensive in processing time for bulk memory devices. For such devices, controlled memory allocation and access techniques offer less costly solutions. Possible solutions as they relate to the various memory types are as follows:

- <u>Core Residue</u>. All core storage can be treated as pages and the pages cleared to zero when allocated, thereby overwriting any potential residue. Via the program's page map, the operating system can label all code and data pages (which need not be contiguous) belonging to a given program with a single hardware memory protection key, thereby prohibiting unauthorized reading or writing by other, potentially co-resident user programs that may be in execution. Further, the operating system can keep a running account of the status and disposition of all pages of core. Unfilled portions of pages at load time can be kept cleared to zero as when they were allocated, and the full page swapped into core, if not already resident, each scheduled time slice. Newly allocated pages can be marked as "changed" pages, as a means of guaranteeing subsequent swap out to drum.

  The foregoing techniques deny access by a user or program to those pages of core not identified as part of his program, and clear core residue by overwriting accessible core at load and swap times.

- <u>Drum Residue</u>. The operating system can always clear a drum page to zero before it is allocated, and maintain a drum map that notes the disposition of all drum pages.

Further, drum input/output (as for all I/O operations) will be controlled by privileged instructions.

- Disk Residue. The expected large capacity of the disk file system makes it infeasible to consider automatic overwriting techniques for residue control. This means that the disk files will necessarily be maintained, in the IMIS, as "dirty" memory. The burden of controlling any unauthorized disk file access, whether to cataloged files or uncataloged disk memory, should be on the IPS/70 Data Management function of the operating system via legality checks of all OPEN and I/O requests. Normal internal labeling of disk packs will assist the legality checking. Scratch memory allocated for new jobs should be written before reading is permitted, to prevent residue access. The act of writing will overwrite the residue and advance the end-of-file (EOF) to prevent reading beyond that point.
- Tape Residue. Tape residue control can be satisfied by manual, off-line degaussing.

Security Control Parameter Safeguards. Security control parameters are the passwords, keys, and associated data employed to control access to the system data base by user programs. The sensitivity of these parameters is evident. They comprise a set of data for which the MIS Department is the Department of Primary Responsibility (DPR) and which must be classified as Highly Restricted. Consistent with this classification, access to these data is further restricted within the department to a very few individuals, carefully selected and trained for the purpose, at the central computer facility.

It is necessary to recognize that the confidentiality classification of these data must be confined to the actual values which reside at any one time in the files and tables. Information about the organization and nature of the control parameters and how they operate is design information which must be determined by, and be subsequently available to, systems analysts/designers, computer programmers, and others. There are sufficient reasons why such information normally carries a Public classification for the IMIS.

As is true of the system data base in general, security measures also apply directly to the access of data values contained in the tables or files at any one time, for purposes of either loading the data initially or making changes. The loading and updating of the system tables and/or files containing the data conducted at the System Administrator's terminal, and the operations are restricted to as few individuals as possible.

Access to the system tables and files containing the parameters is made via a special user ID that is not a member of the set of user

IDs carried in the tables and files. The program or programs making the OPEN call to these tables and files is a member of the set of operating system programs; i.e., it must be executable only in control mode.

Associated problems of security for the data in question relate to keeping backup files as protection against drastic system failures. Any such backup files can be protected through applicable physical and other security measures, e.g., secure storage and transport, and/or of privacy transformations.

3.2.5 Data Handling and Accountability

Special measures taken to protect confidential data and computer programs include those outlined below.

3.2.5.1 Marking of Confidential Data

Conventional typewritten or handwritten documents containing confidential data are stamped with the data classification.

A deck of data processing cards containing confidential data have front and back cover cards stamped with the data classification. Cards removed from the deck for separate processing are subject to special handling and must carry the required markings.

Classification markings on pages of listings produced by automatic data processing equipment are applied by the equipment, with the exception of any ad hoc reports, which are marked manually and packaged in double envelopes.

Tags, stickers, or similar devices are attached to identify the classification of materials that are not easily marked, e.g., tapes and disks.

All file folders, binders, envelopes, metal storage containers, and other containers of confidential information are marked with the classification of their most highly classified content.

3.2.5.2 Accountability of Confidential Data

A system of signed receipts or log signatures is used to control the routing, loaning, disposal, or transfer of confidential data from location to location, from one employee to another, or for returning the data to an issuing agency.

3.2.5.3. Waste Disposal

Such waste material as excess pages of listings, spoilage, ribbons, or carbons is stored in locked containers and destroyed by designated authorized personnel.

3.2.5.4 Storage of Data and Computer Programs

All confidential data, on whatever medium recorded, are stored in containers equipped with combination locks when not in use. A decal is affixed to each container to indicate the classification of the data, the names of persons authorized to have the container combination, and the date the combination was last changed.

All computer programs, regardless of classification, are stored in locked containers when not in use and the names of the persons authorized access to the containers are marked on the container.

3.2.5.5 Reproduction of Confidential Data

Printed reproductions of confidential data occur only when specifically authorized in individual cases. Any copy made is handled by document security control procedures.

3.2.5.6 Purging of Confidential Data

Procedures are developed to ensure that all data no longer needed in the system are subjected to systematic review and purging. In the interests of conserving storage space, as well as for security purposes, measures are enforced to counteract the common tendency to accumulate and maintain data past their useful life.

3.2.6 Emergency Procedures

Emergency situations addressed in this section include those which could arise as a result of occurrences such as the following:
- Bomb Threats
- Civil Disturbances, Disorders, or Demonstrations
- Earthquake
- Fire and/or Explosion
- Serious Industrial Accidents
- Major Power Failures

Potential damage resulting from such occurrences includes losses of property, personal injuries, and interruptions of system operation. These can be minimized through the development of standard procedures, proper advance training, and indoctrination of system personnel. Materials outlined below indicate the approach necessary to deal with those emergency situations. Each of the areas discussed requires extensive amplification and refinement in the course of developing and implementing effective countermeasures.

3.2.6.1   Policy

Examples of general management policy to be formulated and enforced are the following:
- No weapons of any kind will be issued, nor will any IMIS personnel be permitted to bring weapons onto the premises.
- Requests for assistance will be made to the appropriate civil authorities, including local and state law enforcement agencies.
- Employees will make every effort to secure all sensitive material in authorized storage containers.
- Employees will shut off the power to operating machinery and equipment when it is verified that an emergency situation exists.

3.2.6.2   Bomb Threats

Nationwide surveys indicate that industrial firms and municipal buildings are subjected to bomb threats with increasing frequency each year. It is generally impossible to establish the validity of a given threat at the time it is made. However, prompt decisive action is required to obtain all possible information and reduce or eliminate the potential damage, injury, or other loss.

If a bomb threat is received over the telephone, the switchboard operator or person receiving the call should attempt to obtain the following information:
- Originator or source of call
- Location of bomb
- Time set to go off
- Description of bomb: type, shape, color, etc.
- How the bomb was placed in the facility
- How to disarm the bomb

Any person receiving such a call should immediately contact the System Administrator and report the information obtained. The System Administrator notifies appropriate outside authorities and provides all necessary assistance in the investigation of the threat.

3.2.6.3   Civil Disturbances, Disorders, or Demonstrations

If the IMIS facility is confronted with an organized demonstration, civil disturbance, picketing, or protest, procedures must be employed immediately to protect personnel, property and information, prevent or reduce disruption of IMIS operations, and prevent or minimize physical penetration of the facility.

It is likely that any organized disturbance or picketing would take place during normal working hours, with efforts directed toward areas calculated to draw maximum attention from both the public and IMIS personnel.

If there is a demonstration, IMIS policy is to achieve, to the maximum extent possible, a peaceful and orderly demonstration which does not interfere with personnel, property or activities. Such action is appropriate under the circumstances with regard to disorderly or destructive conduct, trespass, or other illegal or harmful activity.

Upon notification that a protest activity or demonstration of any kind is in progress on IMIS system property, the System Administrator should take the following actions:

- Notify the Charlotte Police Department and other appropriate agencies.
- Using personnel available, take up positions which deny unauthorized access to operational areas of the facility.
- If trespass is imminent, assure that all confidential and other valuable material is placed in locked containers or otherwise secured.

Not all anticipated situations will necessarily be militant, violent, or destructive. For example, there is the possibility of being confronted by a peaceful demonstration. However, whether or not there is a serious threat of damage, IMIS personnel should be indoctrinated in such attitudes and procedures as those listed below:

- In the event of a peaceful demonstration, the response should be flexible, considered, and tolerant of the constitutional rights of the demonstrators to freedom of speech, press, or assembly.
- Should a demonstration occur, the protection of confidential and other valuable materials is of primary importance, and instructions are issued to secure all such material. Employees will be cautioned not to approach the scene of action, since it is a good tactic to provide demonstrators with as small an audience as possible.
- Physical or verbal confrontations with threatening demonstrators are to be carefully avoided. Employees who leave the premises to avoid such confrontations are not penalized for loss of time. Employees are afforded appropriate police, legal, or other protection against violence or intimidation. Employees are subject to penalties, including arrest, for engaging in actions which are contrary to these policies, e.g., encouraging confrontations or provoking violence.

3.3   Information Processing System, IPS/70

IPS/70 is a communication transaction-based data management system. Processing is initiated with a transaction from a remote

140

terminal. IPS/70 performs all of the steps required to establish that transaction in the computer and then initiates operation of a user-written program to process the transaction. The user program interfaces with the communications network and the data base via IPS/70 using simple CALL statements. The following paragraphs identify the current IPS/70 security capabilities.

3.3.1 Security Provisions of IPS/70

IPS/70 supports security in two areas: Transaction Processing and Data Base Management. Transaction Processing provides for message-to-terminal association and password techniques to insure proper authorization for program execution. Data Management supports three levels of security: (1) permission to access the file; (2) permission to process the file in a particular manner; and (3) permission to access a particular segment within a file record. IPS/70 provides for an individual locus for controlling system security, which is assigned to the System Administrator. Operating at a privileged terminal, the System Administrator supplies parametric inputs used by IPS/70 to enforce security, and can provide similar information on a need-to-know basis to the terminal users and programmers. Also, the System Administrator can receive reports on attempts to violate the system security and to modify security values.

3.3.1.1 Transaction Processing

The System Administrator furnishes a list of transactions for each terminal and supplies information to the Terminal Directory Generator, which builds a terminal directory defining all transactions Transactions are accepted only from terminals that have been associated with individual transactions and are rejected from terminals that have not been associated. The System Administrator may specify a unique password for a defined transaction and terminal users are then required to supply this password whenever the transaction is generated. The Transaction Control Program rejects a message of this type not containing the proper password, and returns it to the sender with a notation that there was an invalid or missing password. Passwords can be modified on-line by the System Administrator.

The System Administrator may also supply a sender ID, which can be included in the transaction. However, IPS/70 does not validate or use the sender ID for security checking. An "own-code" routine (written in BAL) can be added to intercept messages prior to transaction establishment, to validate sender ID. The user program itself can do this checking, if desired.

An input message from a terminal is in the following format:

```
STX        txcode staserno key [password] [sdsid] text EXT
Where:
           STX       = transmission control character
                       indicating start of transaction
           txcode    = transaction identification code
           staserno  = terminal identification
           key       = 0, no password or sender ID
                     = 1, password only
                     = 2, sender ID only
                     = 3, password and sender ID
           password  = password (optional)
           sdsid     = sender ID (optional)
           text      = text of transaction
           EXT       = transaction control character
                       indicating end of transaction
```

3.3.1.2 Data Base Management

IPS/70 provides a Directory Generator to build a temporary directory to support the data management functions. The System Administrator or a programmer supplies the input to the generator. For each file, the following are required:

- The symbolic name used to reference the file
- The file name as it is to appear on the random access volume(s)
- The access method
- The level of processing: record or segment
- The device types, and their serial numbers, that will contain the file
- The file space requirements to be used when the file is allocated
- The record description and structure.

One (or more) entry in the temporary directory is established for each file. User programs may issue IPS/70 I/O requests for files with entries in the temporary directory. However, there is no security validation for these requests.

The System Administrator is supplied with a dedicated terminal function called "catalog" to transfer the entry from the temporary directory to a permanent directory. Security provisions are available for files with entries in the permanent directory.

After the file is cataloged in the permanent director, a "security" function is provided to the System Administrator terminal to insert passwords into the permanent directory entries. When user programs attach (open) or detach (close) these files, the passwords for them must be supplied with the I/O request. Failure by a user program to supply the proper password will result in denial of file access and a message to the System Administrator. Password information is specified as follows:

C SECF Den, VOID
file password

Where:

C SECF = a literal that defines the function being performed

Den = Directory Entry Name (Similar to file name)

file password = 8-byte password

VOID = indicator that no password is required (can be used to delete a password)

Another security procedure available to the System Administrator, in addition to or instead of the file password, is to insert a list of programs that may access the file into the directory entry. A program requesting access to the file will have its name checked against the list in the directory entry. Attempted access by a program that is not listed will be denied and a message will be transmitted to the System Administrator.

In addition to the program name, the System Administrator may specify the processing options permitted to the listed programs. Whenever a listed program attempts to perform a data base function, IPS/70 Data Control checks the function against the permitted processing options. Violators are denied access and the attempted violation is reported.

Program Security information is supplied from the terminal as follows:

$$C\ SECP\ Den, \begin{bmatrix} ALL \\ program\ name \end{bmatrix} \begin{bmatrix} processing \\ options \end{bmatrix}$$

Where:

C SECP = a literal that defines the function being performed

Den = Directory Entry Name

program name = 6-byte name of program permitted access to the file

ALL = indicates all programs may access the file with the processing options defined

143

processing
options = options permitted to program
accessing the file as follows:
L Load
G Get
R Replace
D Delete
I Insert
A Label Read
P Label Write

IPS/70 does provide some security at the segment level. The prime responsibility is placed on the System Administrator who should release only the names of segments required by the program to its programmer. In attaching (opening) the file the program must specify these segments. IPS/70 does not return any other segment from the opened file to the program; therefore, no accidental release of data is permitted.

3.3.2   Evaluation of IPS/70

Restricting terminals to specific transactions and functions is a significant security and control measure. The inclusion of a password has only limited additional security value. It is apparent that if someone had access to a terminal, it would not be difficult for him to discover the proper password, e.g., by just looking over someone else's shoulder. The major emphasis must be on the administrative and physical control of the use of the terminal.

From a data base standpoint, the most effective procedure is the list of programs permitted to access and process a file. When the functions, i.e., Load, Get, (processing options) to be performed are also specified, this becomes a fairly powerful tool. The password has only limited additional value. The IPS/70 segment sensitivity feature is misleading. It prevents the accidental accessing of sensitive information, but it is no deterrent against someone trying to get information that should not be available. If segment sensitivity could be specified by the System Administrator and contained in the terminal (transaction) directory rather than being input by the user program when it opens a file, it would be most effective (See 3.3.3.)

In summary, although IPS/70 offers some security procedures, the emphasis must be on administrative procedures. This is particularly true as it pertains to the System Administrator and his terminal. From that terminal, actions can be taken to compromise or destroy the entire system. Yet there are no automated security procedures for the System Administrator. Thus, administrative security procedures for the System Administrator, his staff, his office and its contents, and the terminal are matters which must be covered through facility and personnel security measures.

3.3.3 Additional IPS/70 Capability

UNIVAC has stated that IPS/70 does have segment sensitivity at a higher level of sophistication than has been documented They have stated that when the System Administrator, through terminal action, lists the programs which may access a file and the options that may be performed, he may also specify the segments that may be processed by that program. The list of segments supplied by the attach command is validated against this list, and Data Control denies access for segments not defined as accessible. This is a most powerful capability and could become a key feature of the security system. Because of the importance of this capability, and the absence of present documentation, the city will take steps to ascertain (from UNIVAC) its availability for the Charlotte IPS/70.

APPENDIX E

RULES OF ORGANIZATION, PRACTICE AND
PROCEDURE OF THE
WICHITA FALLS DATA ACCESS ADVISORY BOARD

Object of Rules

The purpose of these Rules is to provide for the efficient organization and functioning of, and to provide for a simple and orderly
system of procedure before, the Wichita Falls Data Access Advisory
Board to the end that the public interest and welfare may be protected
and that the business of the Board may be expeditiously handled.

Scope of Rules

These Rules are adopted pursuant to the authority granted by
the Board of Aldermen, City of Wichita Falls, by Ordinance 2688 and
shall govern the organization of the conduct of proceedings of the
Data Access Advisory Board. Such Rules shall not be construed so
as to diminish, modify, or alter the jurisdiction, power, or authority
of the City Manager, as set forth in the Code of Ordinances of the
City of Wichita Falls.

Organization

Appointment of Board and Chairman

The Board shall be composed of five members who shall be
appointed by the Mayor and approved by the Board of Aldermen. The
Mayor, with approval of the Board of Aldermen, shall appoint one
of the members as Chairman.

The Members of the Board shall designate a Vice-Chairman,
who will fulfill the duties of the Chairman in his absence.

Duties of the Chairman

The Chairman shall act as presiding officer for meetings (if in
attendance); shall set the time and place of regular meetings; shall
approve the Agenda for regular meetings; and shall have the authority
to appoint committees from among the membership as deemed

necessary and desirable to foster the efficient and orderly conduct
of its business.

Board Members

The Data Access Advisory Board shall act in an advisory capacity only and shall have the following duties:
a. To advise the Data Registrar and the Board of Aldermen
regarding controls and policies affecting the release of information.
b. To assist the Data Registrar and the Board of Aldermen in
establishing criteria to determine the "need to know" test.
c. To assist the Data Registrar in establishing ethics regarding requests for specific types of information.
d. To consider any expansion of the data base which will result
in acquisition and storage of data not previously maintained
by the City, and to advise the Board of Aldermen with reference
thereto.
Members may recommend items of business for inclusion in
the Agenda of regular meetings of the Board. Such items shall be
submitted to the Secretary not less than five work days prior to each
such meeting.

Ex Officio Member

The Mayor shall appoint one member of the Board of Aldermen
to serve as Ex Officio Member, without vote, to represent the Board
of Aldermen.

Secretary

The Data Registrar shall serve as Secretary Member of the
Board without a vote thereon. He shall:
a. attend all meetings of the Board and of its appointed committees.
b. maintain a record of all activities of the Board and submit
the official Minutes of all regular and special meetings to the
Board of Aldermen and to the Members of the Data Access
Advisory Board as soon as possible.
c. provide the Board with all information necessary for the
performance of its duties.
d. submit a proposed Agenda to the Chairman not less than
five work days prior to each regular meeting and upon approval
shall provide each member with such information as deemed
necessary to the consideration of the Agenda.

e. notify all interested parties of the Agenda and of the time and place of meetings and make such materials and items as pertain to the Agenda available to all interested parties, if possible, prior to the meeting.

f. invite the participation of the principals involved in the Agenda and solicit such evidence as they desire to introduce.

g. coordinate the attendance of staff personnel of the City considered necessary to the business before the Board.

h. introduce each item on the Agenda and present such background information as shall be necessary and shall introduce such witnesses and other parties in interest as may wish to be heard, and,

i. provide such clerical/administrative support as required by the Board in its proceedings.

Procedure

Meetings of the Board will be called by the Chairman or Data Registrar on an ad hoc basis such time as periodic meetings become necessary. Notification of meetings will be mailed.

A quorum shall consist of the majority of the voting members of the Board.

Executive Session:

All regular meetings of the Board shall be open to the public. It is expressly provided, however, that the Chairman shall have the authority to call the meeting into Executive Session for good and sufficient grounds. Following the exercise of such privilege, the Chairman shall reopen the meeting to the public and may announce the results of such Executive Session, which shall be recorded in the Minutes.

Order of Business:

The business to be conducted by the Board at its regular meetings shall be limited to the Agenda. The Chairman shall, however, have the prerogative of waiving this limitation when considered appropriate.

Parties in Interest:

Any interested party may appear or be represented before the Board for the purpose of presenting any relevant and proper testimony and evidence bearing upon the business at hand. Parties wishing to appear or to be so represented should inform the Secretary prior to the date of the meeting; however, the Board may hear anyone present at its discretion.

Order of Procedure:

The Chairman shall direct all parties to enter their appearances on the record.

Adoption of Rules:

These rules were adopted by the Data Access Advisory Board on the day of February 14, 1973, and, subject to approval by the Board of Aldermen, City of Wichita Falls, shall be effective immediately.

Although public concern over the issue of privacy and computerized information systems is relatively new, dating from the debate over the proposal for the creation of a National Data Center in 1966, a considerable body of literature on the subject has been published since the early 1960s. It would be neither feasible nor particularly useful to attempt to list here all that has been published on the subject. What follows is a highly selective bibliography, which we believe includes the most interesting, significant, and useful works that have been published. Annotation of each work has been included to enable the reader to judge his own interest in reading the entire work. For the reader who wishes to pursue the literature even more deeply, references to several other bibliographies are included.

Bibliographies

Harrison, Annette. The Problem of Privacy in the Computer Age: An Annotated Bibliography. Santa Monica, Calif.: the RAND Corporation, 1967.
An excellent, though now outdated, classified and annotated bibliography. Also contains an introductory essay on the problem of privacy in the computer age.

Hoffman, Lance J. "Computers and Privacy: A Survey," Computing Surveys 1 (June 1969): 85.
Discusses privacy briefly and surveys existing and possible proposals for computer security. Discusses research possibilities. Contains an annotated bibliography.

Miller, Arthur R. The Assault on Privacy. Ann Arbor, Mich.: University of Michigan Press, 1971.
An alphabetical listing of major works on privacy and computers, pp. 261-69. Listing is not annotated.

United States Department of Health Education and Welfare, Secretary's Advisory Committee on Automated Personal Data Systems. Records, Computers, and the Rights of Citizens. Washington: U.S. Government Printing Office, 1973.
This Report of the Secretary's Advisory Committee on Automated Personal Data Systems contains an excellent, up-to-date

alphabetical, annotated bibliography on the subject of privacy and computers, pp. 298–330.

Van Tassel, Dennis. Computer Security Management. Englewood Cliffs, N.J.: Prentice–Hall, 1972.
Contains an alphabetical, annotated bibliography on the subject of security in a computer environment, pp. 192–212.

Westin, Alan F., ed. Information Technology in a Democracy. Cambridge, Mass.: Harvard University Press, 1971.
Contains an alphabetical listing of major works on computers and social problems of the computer age, pp. 463–82. Listing is not annotated.

Criminal Justice Systems and Privacy

Fishman, Philip F. "Expungement of Arrest Records: Legislation and Litigation to Prevent Their Abuse," The Clearinghouse Review 6 (April 1973): 725–33.
A survey of the problem of expunging arrest records.

Gallati, Robert R. J. "Criminal Justice Systems and the Right to Privacy," Public Automation, July 1967.
A brief review of the problem of security in a criminal justice system.

Project SEARCH, Committee on Security and Privacy. Security and Privacy Considerations in Criminal History Information Systems Sacramento. California Crime Technological Research Foundation, 1970.
A guide to privacy and security considerations for systems involving interstate exchange of criminal histories. Includes a discussion of problems likely to be encountered in such systems and proposes privacy policies, safeguards, security arrangements, and a code of ethics.

_____ and U.S., Department of Justice, Law Enforcement Assistance Administration. Symposium on Criminal Justice Information and Statistics Systems. New Orleans, October 3–5, 1972.
A comprehensive discussion of problems in criminal justice information systems including police, courts, and corrections.

Dedication

Dial, O. E., ed. "Computers: To Dedicate or Not to Dedicate, That
 is the Question," The Bureaucrat 1 (Winter 1972): 305-78.
 This issue of the journal of the National Capital Area Chapter
 of the American Society for Public Administration is primarily
 devoted to several articles discussing the advantages and dis-
 advantages of dedicated computer systems as opposed to shared
 or integrated information systems.

Doctors and Computers

Curran, William J.; Stearns, Barbara; and Kaplan, Honora. "Privacy,
 Confidentiality and Other Legal Considerations in the Establishment of a Centralized Health-Data System, " New England
 Journal of Medicine 281 (July 31, 1969): 241-48.
 Discusses the legal issues raised in establishing health data
 systems. Discusses codes of ethics, criminal and civil penalties,
 interagency agreements, and a system of public surveillance
 to protect individual privacy and the confidentiality of data.

Olafson, Freya; Ferguson, Allen, Jr.; and Parker, Alberta W. Confidentiality: A Guide for Neighborhood Health Centers. San
 Francisco, Calif.: Pisani Printing Co., 1971.
 A study of the legal and ethical aspects of confidentiality of
 patient information and records maintained by neighborhood
 health centers. Includes applicable state laws from Alabama,
 California, New York, and Ohio.

Ryan, G. A., and Monroe, K. E. Computer Assisted Medical Practice:
 The AMA's Role. Chicago: American Medical Association,
 1971.

Dossiers

"The Computerization of Government Files: What Impact on the
 Individual?" UCLA Law Review 15 (September 1968): 1374-
 1498.
 Discusses the experiences of the California and federal governments in computerizing files and the dangers associated with
 government use of computerized information systems. Suggests
 safeguards to prevent unauthorized disclosure of personal information or disclosure of false or misleading information.

Countryman, Vern. "The Diminishing Right of Privacy: The Personal
   Dossier and the Computer," <u>Texas Law Review</u> 49 (May 1971):
   8-21.
   Lists dossier-compiling activities of private and governmental
   agencies such as the FBI, IRS, Census Bureau, House Internal
   Security Committee, the armed services, credit bureaus,
   investigative reporting agencies, and "punitive compilers."
   Argues that the legislation will not adequately restrict use of
   personal dossiers or protect privacy.

Hoffman, Lance J. and Miller, W. F. "Getting a Personal Dossier
   from a Statistical Data Bank," <u>Datamation</u> 16 (May 1970):
   74-75.
   Demonstrates how a statistical data bank may be used as an
   information data bank resulting in the compiling of personal
   dossiers.

Miller, Arthur R. <u>The Assault on Privacy: Computers, Data Banks,
   and Dossiers</u>. Ann Arbor. University of Michigan Press, 1971.
   Republished as a paperback Signet Book, New York: The
   New American Library, 1972.
   A basic work covering many facets of the problem of privacy
   in the computer age. Surveys law, policy, and practice and
   makes many suggestions for dealing with the issues that are
   raised.

Wheeler, Stanton, ed. <u>On Record: Files and Dossiers in American
   Life</u>. New York. Russell Sage Foundation, 1969.
   Describes record-keeping practices of private and governmental agencies such as schools, credit bureaus, businesses,
   insurance companies, military and security agencies, welfare
   agencies, juvenile courts, mental hospitals, the Census Bureau,
   and the Social Security Administration.

General References on Computers and Privacy

Bisco, Ralph L., ed. <u>Data Bases, Computers, and the Social Sciences</u>.
   New York: Wiley-Interscience, 1970.
   A selection of papers from the conference of the Council of
   Social Science Data Archives at UCLA in June 1967. Some of
   the technical articles are quite useful.

Clark, John O. E. <u>Computers at Work.</u> New York: Bantam Books,
   Grosset & Dunlap, 1973.

Describes applications of computers that affect people and their work.

Greenberger, Martin, ed. Computers, Communications, and the Public Interest. Baltimore: John Hopkins University Press, 1971.
A collection of papers that examine the problems of preserving traditional human rights and values in view of increasing reliance on computer technology.

Packard, Vance. The Naked Society. New York: David McKay Co., 1964.
A popularized presentation of an exposé of government and big business snooping into the private lives of citizens.

Pylyshyn, Zenon W., ed. Perspectives on the Computer Revolution. Englewood Cliffs, N.J.: Prentice-Hall, 1970.
"The book is divided conceptually into three parts. The first is devoted to the development of computers and the intellectual heritage of computer science. The second part emphasizes the relationship between man—as a conscious thinking organism--and machines. The last part bears primarily on the relationship between society as a whole and the machine."

Sackman, Harold and Boehm, Barry W. Planning Community Information Utilities. Montvale, N.J.: AFIPS Press, 1972.
Discusses the development of computer-based mass information utilities. Part IV contains articles dealing with its control:
Nanus, Burt. "The Municipal Framework."
Rivkin, Steven R.: "Creating Community Information Utilities—the Regulatory Problem."
Goldberg, Edward M.: "Consumer Safeguards."
Gilchrist, Bruce. "Public Involvement and Acceptance."

Taviss, Irene, ed. The Computer Impact. Englewood Cliffs, N.J.: Prentice-Hall, 1970.
A collection of papers that consider the issues raised by the application of computer technology to the political decision-making process and to the economy.

United States, Department of Health, Education and Welfare. Records, Computers and the Rights of Citizens. Washington: U.S. Government Printing Office, 1973.
Report of the Secretary's Advisory Committee on Automated Personal Data Systems. Central concern is the relationship

between individuals and record-keeping organizations. Identifies
key issues and makes specific recommendations for action.

Westin, Alan F., ed. <u>Information Technology in a Democracy</u>. Cambridge, Mass: Harvard Unversity Press, 1971.
A collection of approximately fifty papers relating to the use
of information technology in the political decision-making
process.

_____. <u>Privacy and Freedom</u>. New York: Atheneum, 1967
A seminal work on the implications of surveillance technologies
for personal privacy.

_____ and Baker, Michael A. <u>Databanks in a Free Society</u>. New
York: Quadrangle Books, 1972.
Report of the National Academy of Sciences Project on Computer
Databanks. A nationwide, in-depth study of what the use of
computers is actually doing to record-keeping processes and
what the growth of large-scale data banks means for the citizen's
rights to privacy and due process. Suggests public policy actions
to regulate the use of data banks.

Law of Privacy

Ernst, Morris L., and Schwartz, Alan U. <u>Privacy: the Right to Be
Let Alone</u>. New York: Macmillan Co., 1962.
Written for the layman, describes major cases in the development of the law on privacy. Good background, but now not up-
to-date.

Fried, Charles. "Privacy," <u>Yale Law Journal</u> 77 (January 1968):
475-93.
Discussion of privacy law.

Loth, David, and Ernst, Morris L. <u>The Taming of Technology</u>. New
York: Simon and Schuster, 1972.
Describes legal means of controlling potentially harmful aspects
of technology. Includes proposals for regulation of data banks.

Medlman, Jeffrey A. "Centralized Information Systems and the Legal
Right to Privacy," <u>Marquette Law Review</u> 52 (1969): 335-54.
Discusses the law of privacy with specific reference to com-
puterized information systems.

Michael, Donald N. "Speculations on the Relation of the Computer to Individual Freedom and the Right to Privacy," George Washington Law Review 33 (1964): 270-86.
An early essay discussing the law of privacy with specific reference to computerized information systems.

Prosser, William H. "Privacy," California Law Review 48 (August 1960): 383-423.
An essay on the law of privacy by the leading authority on tort law in the United States. Although now somewhat out-of-date, this is still a valuable article.

Warren, Samual D. and Brandeis, Louis D. "The Right to Privacy," Harvard Law Review 4 (December 1890): 193-220.
The seminal work arguing for the recognition of privacy as a legal right with legal remedies when that right is abridged. A classic work.

Lawyers and Computers

American Bar Association, Standing Committee of Law and Technology. Computers and the Law. Edited by Robert P. Bigelow. 2d edition. New York: Commerce Clearinghouse, Inc., 1969.
Lists the use of computers by lawyers. Also includes articles on the problem of data banks and privacy; on federal regulation of computers; and on computer-based criminal justice information systems.

Bigelow, Robert P., ed. Computer Law Service. Chicago: Callaghan & Company, 1972.
"The purpose of the Computer Law Service is to provide the practicing lawyer with explanatory articles, reference materials, and the decisions of courts and agencies that will help him handle the legal problems that have been raised by the invention and use of the computer.

Privacy

Columbia University. Columbia Human Rights Law Review 4 (Winter 1972): 1.
Entire issue devoted to debate on privacy. Articles include:
    Miller, Arthur R. "Computers, Data Banks and Individual Privacy: an Overview."

Ervin, Sam J., Jr. "The First Amendment: A Living
Thought in the Computer Age."
Katzenbach, Nicholas de B., and Tome, Richard W.
"Crime Data Centers: The Use of Computers in
Crime Detection and Prevention."
Askin, Frank. "Surveillance: The Social Science Per-
spective."
Baker, Michael A. "Record Privacy as a Marginal
Problem: The Limits of Consciousness and Concern."
Flannery, John P. "Commercial Information Brokers."

Duke University, School of Law. "Privacy," Law and Contemporary
Problems 31 (Spring 1966): 2.
Entire Issue devoted to debate on privacy. Articles include:
Beany, William M. "The Right of Privacy and American
Law."
Konvitz, Milton R. "Privacy and the Law: A Philosophical
Prelude."
Shils, Edward. "Privacy: Its Constitution and Vicis-
situdes."
Jourard, Sidney M. "Some Psychological Aspects of
Privacy."
Kalven, Harry Jr. "Privacy in Tort Law—Were Warren
and Brandeis Wrong?"
Karst, Kenneth L. " 'The Files': Legal Controls Over
the Accuracy and Accessibility of Stored Personal
Data."
Handler, Joel F., and Rosenheim. "Privacy in Welfare:
Public Assistance Juvenile Justice."
Creech, William A. "The Privacy of Government Em-
ployees."

Lusky, Louis. "Invasion of Privacy: A Clarification of Concepts."
Political Science Quarterly 87 (June 1972): 192-209.
Criticizes a unitary definition of privacy. Argues that the
formulation of legislation protecting privacy must be preceded
by a consideration of the existence of two types of information
transfer: the transfer of personal information against the will
of the individual and the transfer of false or misleading information about an individual.

Pastalan, Leon A. "Privacy as a Behavioral Concept," Social Science
45 (April 1972): 93-117.
"The purpose of this paper is to propose an operational definition of privacy; and to derive potential research payoffs through

the use of a matrix model linking the various modes of privacy
to a series of related situational contingencies."

Pennock, J. Roland, and Chapman, John W., eds. Privacy. New
York: Atherton Press, 1971.
A collection of essays discussing the concept of privacy from
several different perspectives.

Rosenberg, Jerry M. The Death of Privacy. New York: Random
House, 1969.
An empirical study of the meaning of privacy.

"Symposium: Computers, Data Banks, and Individual Privacy,"
Minnesota Law Review 53 (December 1968): 211-45.
Lectures from a symposium sponsored by the Merrill Cohen
Memorial Fund and the Graduate School of Business Administra-
tion, University of Minnesota. Articles include:
    Ruggles, Richard. "On the Needs and Values of Data
    Banks."
    Pemberton, John deJ., Jr. "On the Dangers, Legal
    Aspect, and Remedies."
    Miller, Arthur R. "On Proposals and Requirements
    for Solutions."

"Symposium on Privacy and the Law," University of Illinois Law
Forum, 1971, 137-78,
Three papers presented at the University of Illinois College of
Law, May 7, 1971. Articles Include:
    Ervin, Sam J., Jr. "Privacy and Government Investiga-
    tions."
    Miller, Arthur R. "The Dossier Society."
    Harrington, Michael. "Privacy and the Poor."

Privacy Issues in Countries Other than the
United States

Breckenridge, Adam C. The Right to Privacy. Lincoln: University
of Nebraska Press, 1970.
A discussion of privacy cases in Great Britain and the United
States.

British Computer Society. Privacy and the Computer—Steps to
Practicality. Edited by L. Ellis. London: British Computer
Society, 1972.
A statement of the British professionals' view of the privacy
problem.

Canada, Department of Communications and Department of Justice.
    Privacy and Computers. Ottawa: Information Canada, 1972.
    Report of the Task Force on Privacy and Computers established
    by the Departments of Communications and Justice in 1971.
    Includes a study of the value of privacy, a summary of empirical
    studies of the state of information processing in Canada in both
    the private and public sectors, and an analysis of the legal
    system and the protection of privacy.

_____. _Statistical Data Banks and Their Effects on Privacy_.
    Ottawa: Information Canada, 1972.
    A study by H. S. Gellman prepared for the Task Force on
    Privacy and Computers.

Cortes, Irene R. _The Constitutional Foundations of Privacy_. Quezon
    City: The University of Philippines Law Center, 1970.
    A discussion of the nature of privacy and of the development of
    the concept of privacy as a tort and in constitutional law in
    Great Britain, the Philippines, and the United States.

Federal Republic of Germany, Hesse State Parliament, Data Protec-
    tion Commissioner. _First Activity Report_. Document 7/1495
    (1972).
    Evaluates the weaknesses of the Hesse Data Protection Act.
    Describes the development of data processing and of the legal
    regulation of access to personal information in administrative
    records in the several German Lander, in the Federal Govern-
    ment of Germany, in France, in the United States, and in the
    United Kingdom. Makes recommendations for specific safe-
    guards.

_____. _Second Activity Report_, Document 7/3137 (1973).
    Discusses developments in the second year of operation of the
    Hesse Data Protection Act.

Great Britain, Home Office. _Report of the Committee on Privacy_.
    London: Her Majesty's Stationery Office, 1972.
    The final report of the committee chaired by the Right Honorable
    Kenneth Younger. Established in 1970 to review the need for
    legislation to protect "individuals and commercial and indus-
    trial interests" from invasion of privacy, the report examines
    the nature of privacy, complaints of invasion of privacy, the
    adequacy of existing law in protecting against invasions of
    privacy, the disclosure of confidential information, and the
    creation of a general right to privacy.

159

_____, House of Commons Library Research Division. Reference Sheet: Privacy, Ref. 69/7 (March 4, (1969).
A list of newspaper and periodical articles, publications of the National Council for Civil Liberties, parliamentary material, and law relating to privacy.

International Commission of Jurists. "The Protection of Privacy," International Social Science Journal 24 (1972): 3.
A comparative survey of the legal protection of privacy in ten countries: Argentina, Brazil, the Federal Republic of Germany, France, Mexico, Sweden, Switzerland, the United Kingdom, the United States, and Venezuela.

Justice (British Section of the International Commission of Jurists). Privacy and the Law. London: Stevens & Sons, Ltd., 1970.
Discusses the law relating to privacy in England, France, Germany, and the United States.

Niblett, G. B. F. Digital Information and the Privacy Problem. Paris: Organization for Economic Cooperation and Development, 1971.
Examines problems of data confidentiality and computerized information systems in OECD nations. Discusses professional standards, technological safeguards, administrative practices, legal remedies and sanctions, and new legislation. Includes a summary of OECD nation replies to a questionnaire on privacy.

Rowe, B. C., ed. Privacy, Computers and You. Manchester: The National Computing Centre Ltd., 1972.
A collection of papers presented at the Workshop on the Data Bank Society, London, 1970, sponsored by the National Council for Civil Liberties and Allan Unwin Ltd. Includes papers on privacy in a technological society; on the use of data banks by physicians, psychologists, banks, and credit bureaus; on trade unions and data banks; and on proposals for technical, legal, and ethical safeguards of privacy.

Rule, James B. Private Lives and Public Surveillance. London: Allen Lane, 1973
Considers the use of personal information as a means of social control. The record-keeping activities involved in police record systems, vehicle and driver licensing, National Insurance in Great Britain, and consumer credit and the BankAmericard systems in the United States are analyzed.

Stromholm, Stig. Right of Privacy and Rights of Personality: A Comparative Survey. Working paper prepared for the Nordic Conference on Privacy organized by the International Commission of Jurists, Stockholm, May 1967. Stockholm: P. A. Norstedt & Soners Forlag, 1967.
A study directed to the question of "how to define and protect a person's legitimate interest in being . . . let alone." Examines the nature of privacy and legal rules, legislative initiatives, and standards of private organizations for protecting privacy.

Professional Associations' Codes of Ethics, Procedures, and Statements

American Anthropological Association. "Principles of Professional Responsibility." Adopted by the Council of the American Anthropological Association, Washington, D.C., May 1971.

American Association for Public Opinion Research. "Code of Professional Ethics and Practices," New York: American Association for Public Opinion Research, 1970.

American Civil Liberties Union. Policy Guide. New York: American Civil Liberties Union, 1967.

American Council on Education, Office of Research. "Users' Manual: ACE Higher Education Data Bank," ACE Research Reports 4 (1969): 1.

American Hospital Association. "Statement on a Patient's Bill of Rights," Chicago: American Hospital Association, November 17, 1972.

American Institutes for Research. The Project TALENT Data Bank: A-Handbook. Palo Alto, Calif.: American Institutes for Research, 1972.

American National Standards Institute. ANSI Standard: Identification of Individuals for Information Interchange. New York: American National Standards Institute, 1969.

American Psychiatric Association. "Position Statement on the Need for Preserving Confidentiality of Medical Records in any Health Care System," American Journal of Psychiatry 128 (April 1972): 169.

American Psychological Association, Ad Hoc Committee on Ethical Standards in Psychological Research. Ethical Principles in the Conduct of Research with Human Participants. Washington: American Psychological Association, 1973.

American Sociological Association, Committee on Information Technology and Privacy. "Report of the Committee on Information Technology and Privacy," American Sociologist 5 (November 1970): 409-11.

American Statistical Association. "Maintaining the Professional Integrity of Federal Statistics: A Report of the American Statistical Association—Federal Statistics Users Conference Committee on the Integrity of Federal Statistics," American Statistician 27 (April 1973): 58-67.

Association of Computer Programmers and Analysts. "The Data Bank and Your Privacy: The ACPA's Position," Newsletter of the Association of Computer Programmers and Analysts, September-October 1970.

California, State of. Intergovernmental Board on Electronic Data Processing. Policy Statement on Privacy and Security. Sacramento, Calif.: State Printing Office, 1971.

Data Processing Management Association. "Codes of Conduct and Good Practice for CDP Holders to be Developed by Certification Council," News Release, Chicago, May 1972.

Massachusetts Institute of Technology. Final Report of the Ad Hoc Committee on the Privacy of Information at MIT. Cambridge: Massachusetts Institute of Technology, 1971.

National Accreditation Council for Agencies Serving the Blind and Visually Handicapped. "Standards for Confidentiality," New York, April 1972.

National Council on Crime and Delinquency. "Bay Area Counties Research Project: Proposed Security and Privacy Procedures for Information Collected," Hackensack, N.J., n.d.

_____. "Security and Privacy in the Parole Decision-Making Project," Hackensack, N.J., n.d.

_____. "Security and Privacy in the Uniform Parole Reports Program." Hackensack, N.J., n.d.

National League for Nursing. "Policy and Procedures Regarding
Research Investigations Involving Human Subjects," New York,
revised, March 1969.

National Social Welfare Assembly, Ad Hoc Committee on Confidentiality
Confidentiality in Social Service to Individuals. New York:
National Social Welfare Assembly, 1958.

Russell Sage Foundation. "Guidelines for the Collection, Maintenance
and Dissemination of Pupil Records." Report of a Conference
on the Ethical and Legal Aspects of School Record Keeping,
Sterling Forest, N.Y., May 25-28, 1969.

_____. Student Records in Higher Education: Recommendations
for the Formulation and Implementation of Record-Keeping
Policies in Colleges and Universities. New York: the Foundation, 1973.

Social Science Research Council. Report of the Committee on the
Preservation and Use of Economic Data to the Social Science
Research Council. New York: the Council, 1965.

Stanford University. Report of the Ad Hoc Committee on Protection
of Privacy of Information at Stanford. Stanford, Calif.: Stanford University Press, 1972.

Security, Auditing, and Control

Brown, William F., ed. AMR's Guide to Computer and Software
Security. New York: AMR International, Inc., 1971.
A complete guide to the problems of computer and software
security, including methods of dealing with the problems.
Contains planning guides and checklists.

International Business Machines. The Considerations of Security in
a Computer Environment. White Plains, N.Y.: IBM, n.d.

Jancura, Elise G., and Berger, Arnold H. Computers: Auditing and
Control. Philadelphia, Auerbach, 1973.

Parker, Donn B., et al. Computer Abuse: Financial Report. SRI
Project, ISU 2501, NSF Grant No. GI-37226, Stanford Research
Institute, November 1973.

Summarizes and analyses 148 reported cases of computer abuse from technical, legal, and sociological perspectives. Purpose is to alert government users of computers of the seriousness of the problem.

Van Tassel, Dennis. Computer Security Management. Englewood Cliffs, N.J.: Prentice-Hall, 1972.
A study of the problems of security in computer operation and procedures. Provides guidelines for implementing a complete security system for a computer center.

Urban Information Systems

Dial, O. E. Urban Information Systems: A Bibliographical Essay. Cambridge, Mass: Urban Systems Laboratory, Massachusetts Institute of Technology, 1968.
A comprehensive discussion of the existing literature about urban information systems.

Fogarty, Michael S. Issues of Privacy and Security in the Urban Information System. Portland, Oregon: Northwest Educational Laboratory, 1969.
Surveys the problems of privacy and security in urban information systems and discusses them within the context of developments in the Portland metropolitan area.

Goldberg, Edward M. "Urban Information Systems and Invasions of Privacy," Urban Affairs Quarterly, March 1970, pp. 249-64.
Raises issues of privacy within the specific context of the development of integrated urban information systems.

_____. Privacy Problems in Municipal Information Systems. Claremont, Calif.: Municipal Systems Research, Claremont Graduate School, 1972.
Discusses the conflict between the "right to know" and the "right to privacy." Outlines specific problems concerning privacy in urban information systems and suggests methods of dealing with those problems.

Hearle, Edward F. R., and Mason, Raymond J. A Data Processing System for State and Local Governments. Englewood Cliffs, N.J.: Prentice-Hall, 1963.
A seminal work on the application of computers to state and local governments.

164

Kraemer, Kenneth L. "The Evolution of Information Systems for
    Urban Administration," Public Administration Review 29
    (1969): 389-402.
    Discusses the development of urban information systems.

_____. "USAC: An Evolving Governmental Mechanism for Urban
    Information Systems Development," Public Administration
    Review 31 (1971): 543-51.
    Discusses the activities of the federal government's Urban
    Information Systems Inter-Agency Committee (USAC) in assisting
    local governments in the development of integrated information
    systems.

_____; Mitchel, William H.; Weiner, Myron E.; and Dial, O. E.
    Integrated Municipal Information Systems: The Use of the
    Computer in Local Government. New York: Praeger Publishers,
    1974.
    A complete discussion of USAC, the IMIS program, and the
    state of the art of municipal information systems today.

Mindlin, Albert. "Confidentiality and Local Information Systems,"
    Public Administration Review 28 (1968): 509-18.
    Points out differences in problems of privacy between federal
    and local government information systems and presents a
    program for maintaining confidentiality in local systems.

"USAC: Federal Funding for Municipal Information Systems," Govern-
    ment Data Systems, July-August 1971, pp. 4-7, 22-24.
    Describes the USAC project.

                        Welfare and Privacy

Elias, Stephan R., and Rucker, Trudy. "Knowledge is Power: Poverty
    Law and the Freedom of Information Act," Clearinghouse Re-
    view 6 (May 1972): 1-15.
    Discusses exemptions in the Freedom of Information Act and
    their implications for the release of records to poverty lawyers.

O.E. DIAL is Professor of Public Affairs, Graduate School of Public Affairs, University of Colorado; and Research Professor, University Center, Long Island University. He has served as Senior Consultant to the Federal Interagency Committee on Urban Information Systems (USAC) since 1969.

Professor Dial has published a number of articles and books, including one Praeger Special Series title (as co-author with Kraemer, et. al.), Integrated Municipal Information Systems.

Dr. Dial earned his Ph.D. in Government at Claremont Graduate School, has done advanced work while a visiting professor at MIT, and has been the beneficiary of grants for research work as Director, Municipal Information Systems Research Project since 1970.

EDWARD M. GOLDBERG is a Professor of Political Science and Chairman of the Department of Political Science at California State University, Los Angeles. During recent years he has served as a consultant on privacy questions to the Urban Information Systems Inter-Agence Committee (USAC) of the United States Department of Housing and Urban Development and to Municipal Information Systems Research Project of Long Island University.

Professor Goldberg has published twenty monographs and articles, including Privacy Problems in Municipal Information Systems (Claremont, Ca.: Municipal Systems Research, 1972).

Dr. Goldberg earned his Ph.D. in Political Science at the University of Pennsylvania. He has served as a visiting professor at the University of Southern California, San Diego State University, and the University of New Mexico.

BUDGETING MUNICIPAL EXPENDITURES: A
Study in Comparative Policy Making
Lewis B. Friedman

COMMUNITY DEVELOPMENT STRATEGIES:
Case Studies of Major Model Cities
George J. Washnis

FEDERAL GRANTS TO LOCAL GOVERNMENT
Richard D. Bingham

INTEGRATED MUNICIPAL INFORMATION SYS-
TEMS: The Use of the Computer in Local Gov-
ernment
Kenneth L. Kraemer, William H.
Mitchel, Myron E. Weiner, and O. E.
Dial

LOCAL GOVERNMENT PROGRAM BUDGETING:
Theory and Practice
Werner Z. Hirsch, Sidney Sonenblum,
and Ronald K. Teeples

A PLANNING, PROGRAMMING, AND BUDGET-
ING MANUAL: Resource Allocation in Public Sec-
tor Economies
James Cutt